www.valdebooks.com - 2009

A Narrative of some of the Lord's Dealings with George Müller Written by Himself. Second Part

by

George Müller

TABLE OF CONTENTS

PREFACE TO THE FIRST
EDITION OF THE SECOND PART.

THROUGH grace I am, in some measure, conscious of my many weaknesses and deficiencies; but, with all this, I know that I am a member of the body of Christ, and that, as such, I have a place of service in the body. The realization of this has laid upon me the responsibility of serving the church in the particular way for which the Lord has fitted me, and this has led me to write this second little volume, if by any means those of my fellow-saints, who have not yet learned the importance and preciousness of dealing with God Himself under all circumstances, may be helped in learning this lesson. Nor did I think that the first part of this Narrative rendered the second part needless, because that contains more especially the Lord's dealings with me as an individual, whilst this gives, more particularly, an account of the remarkable way in which the Lord has helped me in reference to His work in my hands. For this second part carries on the account of the Orphan-Houses, etc., which are under my care, and contains the substance of the Reports previously published, so that any one who wishes to have the account from the beginning up to the end of last year, may be able to obtain it. This latter point alone made it needful for me to think about publishing this second part, as of the Reports for 1838 and 1839, which still almost daily are inquired after, there are only a few copies left, though 2,500 of the one and 3,000 of the other were published and of the Report for 1840 there are also only about 500, out of 4,000, remaining. The being thus able to put the whole account of the work into the hands of an inquiring individual, affords such a one a fairer opportunity of seeing the working of those scriptural principles on which the Institution is established. And, lastly, the Lord's continued blessing upon the first part of the Narrative and the Reports, both to believers and unbelievers, has induced me to publish this second volume, which I now affectionately commend to the prayers of the saints, requesting at the same time their prayers for myself.

GEORGE MULLER.

Bristol, June 14, 1841.

SECOND PART

In publishing the continuation of the Narrative of some of the Lord's dealings with me, I have thought it well to give it in the same form in which the larger portion of the former part is written. I therefore proceed to give extracts from my journal making here and there such remarks as occasion may seem to require. The first, part of the Narrative was carried on to the beginning of July 1837, from which period the Continuation commences.

July 18, 1837. Four trials came upon me this morning, without my having previously had opportunity for secret prayer. I had been prevented from rising early, on account of having to spend part of the night in a sick chamber; but this circumstance shows, how important it is to rise early, when we are able, in order that we may be prepared, by communion with the Lord, to meet the trials of the day.

Aug. 15. Today the first 500 copies of my Narrative arrived, and I had, once more, some conflict of mind whether, after all, I had not been mistaken in this matter. A sort of trembling came over me, and a wish to be able to retrace the step. Judging, however, from the most searching self-examination, through which I had caused my heart to pass again and again, as to my motives, before I began writing, and whilst I was writing; and judging, moreover, from the earnestness in prayer with which I had sought to ascertain the mind of God in the matter, and from the subsequent full assurance which I had had of its being according to His will, that in this way I should serve the Church;--I was almost immediately led to consider this uncomfortable and trying feeling as a temptation, and I therefore went to the box, opened it, brought out some copies, and soon after gave away one, so that the step could not be retraced. [This was the last temptation or struggle I have had of that kind; for, though, very many times since, I have had abundant reason for praising the Lord that He put such an honour upon me, in allowing me to speak well of His name in so public a manner, I have never since, even for one minute, been allowed to regret publishing the Narrative; and almost daily have I been more and more confirmed in the conviction, that the giving such like publications to the church, making known the Lord's dealings with me, is one part of my service towards the saints.]

Aug. 17. Today two more children were received into the Infant Orphan-House, which makes up our full number, 66 in the Girls' and infant-Orphan-Houses.

Aug. 28. When brother Craik and I began to labour in Bristol, and consequently some believers united with us in fellowship, assembling together at Bethesda, we began meeting together on the basis of the written Word only, without having any church rules whatever. From the commencement it was understood, that, as the

1

Lord should help us, we would try everything by the word of God, and introduce and hold fast that only which could be proved by Scripture. When we came to this determination on Aug. 13, 1832, it was indeed in weakness, but it was in uprightness of heart.--On account of this it was, that, as we ourselves were not fully settled as to whether those only who had been baptized after they had believed, or whether all who believed in the Lord Jesus, irrespective of baptism, should be received into fellowship nothing was determined about this point. We felt free to break bread and be in communion with those who were not baptized, and therefore could with a good conscience labour at Gideon, where the greater part of the saints, at least at first, were unbaptized; but, at the same time, we had a secret wish that none but believers who were baptized might be united with us at Bethesda. Our reason for this was, that we had witnessed in Devonshire much painful disunion, resulting, as we thought, from baptized and unbaptized believers being in fellowship. Without, then, making it a rule, that Bethesda Church was to be one of close communion, we nevertheless took care that those who applied for fellowship should be instructed about baptism. For many months there occurred no difficulty, as none applied for communion but such as had either been already baptized, or wished to be, or who became convinced of the Scriptural character of believers' baptism, after we had conversed with them; afterwards, however, three sisters applied for fellowship, none of whom had been baptized; nor were their views altered, after we had conversed with them. As, nevertheless, brother Craik and I considered them true believers, and we ourselves were not fully convinced what was the mind of the Lord in such a case, we thought it right that these sisters should be received; yet so that it might be unanimously, as all our church acts then were done; but we knew by that time, that there were several in fellowship with us, who could not conscientiously receive unbaptized believers. We mentioned, therefore, the names of these three sisters to the church, stating that they did not see believers' baptism to be scriptural, and that, if any brother saw, on that account, a reason why they should not be received, he should let us know. The result was, that several objected, and two or three meetings were held, at which we heard the objections of the brethren, and sought for ourselves to obtain acquaintance with the mind of God on the point. Whilst several days thus passed away before the matter was decided, one of those three sisters came and thanked us, that we had not received her, before being baptized, for she now saw that it was only shame and the fear of man which had kept her back, and that the Lord had now made her willing to be baptized. By this circumstance those brethren, who considered it scriptural that all ought to be baptized before being received into fellowship, were confirmed in their views; and as to brother Craik and me, it made us, at least, still more question, whether, those brethren might not be right; and we felt therefore, that in such a state of mind we could not oppose them. The one sister, therefore, who wished to be baptized, was received into fellowship, but the two others not. Our consciences were the less affected by this, because all, though not baptized, might take the Lord's supper with us, at Bethesda, though not be received into full fellowship; and because at Gideon, where there were baptized and unbaptized believers, they might even be received into full fellowship; for we had not then clearly seen that there is no scriptural distinction between being in fellowship with individuals and breaking

2

bread with them. Thus matters stood for many months, i.e. believers were received to the breaking of bread even at Bethesda, though not baptized, but they were not received to all the privileges of fellowship.--In August of 1836 I had a conversation with brother H. C. on the subject of receiving the unbaptized into communion, a subject about which, for years, my mind had been more or less exercised. This brother put the matter thus before me: either unbaptized believers come under the class of persons who walk disorderly, and, in that case, we ought to withdraw from them (2 Thess. iii. 6); or they do not walk disorderly. If a believer be walking disorderly, we are not merely to withdraw from him at the Lord's table, but our behaviour towards him ought to be decidedly different from what it would be were he not walking disorderly, on all occasions when we may have intercourse with him, or come in any way into contact with him, Now this is evidently not the case in the conduct of baptized believers towards their unbaptized fellow-believers. The Spirit does not suffer it to be so, but He witnesses that their not having been baptized does not necessarily imply that they are walking disorderly; and hence there may be the most precious communion between baptized and unbaptized believers. The Spirit does not suffer us to refuse fellowship with them in prayer, in reading and searching the Scriptures, in social and intimate intercourse, and in the Lord's work; and yet this ought to be the case, were they walking disorderly.--This passage, 2 Thess. iii. 6, to which brother R. C. referred, was the means of showing me the mind of the Lord on the subject, which is, that we ought to receive all whom Christ has received (Rom. xv. 7), irrespective of the measure of grace or knowledge which they have attained unto.--Some time after this conversation, in May 1837, an opportunity occurred, when we (for brother Craik had seen the same truth) were called upon to put into practice the light which the Lord had been pleased to give us. A sister, who neither had been baptized, nor considered herself under any obligation to be baptized, applied for fellowship. We conversed with her on this as on other subjects, and proposed her for fellowship, though our conversation had not convinced her that she ought to be baptized. This led the church again to the consideration of the point. We gave our reasons, from Scripture, for considering it right to receive this unbaptized sister to all the privileges of the children of God; but a considerable number, one-third perhaps, expressed conscientious difficulty in receiving her. The example of the Apostles in baptizing the first believers upon a profession of faith, was especially urged, which indeed would be an insurmountable difficulty, had not the truth been mingled with error for so long a time, so that it does not prove willful disobedience, if any one in our day should refuse to be baptized after believing. The Lord, however, gave us much help in pointing out the truth to the brethren, so that the number of those, who considered that only baptized believers should be in communion, decreased almost daily. At last, only fourteen brethren and sisters out of above 180, thought it right, this Aug. 28, 1837, to separate from us, after we had had much intercourse with them. [I am glad to be able to add, that, even of these 14, the greater part afterwards saw their error, and came back again to us, and that the receiving of all who love our Lord Jesus into full communion, irrespective of baptism, has never been the source of disunion among us, though more than forty-four years have passed away since.]

Sept. 2. I have been looking about for a house for the Orphan Boys, these last three days. Every thing else has been provided. The Lord has given suitable individuals to take care of the children, money, &c. In His own time He will give a house also.

Sept. 6. This morning I accompanied a sister, who had been staying a night with us, to the steamer. In answer to prayer I awoke at the right time, the fly came at half-past five, her trunk was got from the vessel in which she came yesterday, and we arrived before the steamer had left. In all these four points I felt my dependence upon the Lord, and He, having put prayer into my heart, answered it in each of these four particulars.

Sept. 15. This evening we had a meeting for inquirers and applicants for fellowship. There were more than we could see within three hours; and when all strength was gone, we had to send away four. Among those whom we saw was E. W., who had been kept for some time from applying for fellowship, on account of not seeing believers' baptism to be scriptural. She wished to be taught, but could not see it. She felt grieved that on that account she could not attend to the breaking of bread, which she did see to be scriptural. As soon as open communion was brought about at Bethesda, she wished to offer herself for fellowship, but was twice prevented by circumstances from doing so. Last Wednesday evening she came to the baptizing, when once more, after the lapse of more than two years, I preached on baptism, which fully convinced her of its being scriptural, and she desires now to be baptized. Her difficulty was, that she thought she had been baptized with the Spirit, and therefore needed no water baptism, which now, from Acts x. 44-47, she sees to be an unscriptural objection.--Though it is only one month this day since my Narrative was published, I have already heard of many instances in which the Lord has been pleased to bless it.

This morning we received a parcel with clothes and some money for the Orphans, from a sister at a distance. Among the donations in money was a little legacy, amounting to 6s. 6 1/2d. from a dear boy, the nephew of the sister who sent the things, who died in the faith. This dear child had had given to him, in his last illness, some new shillings, sixpences, and other smaller silver coins, amounting to the above-mentioned little sum. Shortly before he fell asleep, he requested that this his little treasure might be sent to the Orphans. This precious little legacy is the first we have had.

Sept. 19. Two things were today particularly impressed upon my heart, and may the Lord deepen the impression. 1. That I ought to seek for more retirement, though the work should apparently suffer ever so much. 2. That arrangements should be made, whereby I may be able to visit the brethren more, as an unvisited church will sooner or later become an unhealthy church. Pastors, as fellow-labourers, are greatly needed among us.

Sept. 28, I have for a long time been too much outwardly engaged. Yesterday morning I spent about three hours in the vestry of Gideon, to be able to have more time for retirement. I meant to do the same in the afternoon, but before I could leave the house I was called on, and thus one person after the other came, till I had to go out. Thus it has been again today.

Oct. 16. For a long time past brother Craik and I have felt the importance of more pastoral visiting, and it has been one of our greatest trials, that we have been unable to give more time to it. This evening we had purposely a meeting of the two Churches, at which brother Craik and I spoke on; I. The importance of pastoral visiting. II. The particular obstacles which hindered us in attending to it. III. The question whether there was any way of removing some of the obstacles.

I. As to the importance of pastoral visiting, the following points were mentioned: 1. Watching over the saints, by means of visiting them, to prevent coldness, or to recover them from backsliding. 2. To counsel and advise them in family affairs, in their business, and in spiritual matters. 3. To keep up that loving familiar intercourse, which is so desirable between the saints and those who have the oversight of them.-- These visits should be, if possible, frequent; but in our case there have been several obstacles in the way.

II. The particular obstacles in our case are: 1. The largeness of the number who are in communion with us. One hundred would be quite as many as we have strength to visit regularly, and as often as would be desirable; but there are nearly 400 in fellowship with us. 2. The distance of the houses of the saints from our own dwellings, as many live more than two miles of. 3. The Lord's blessing upon our labours. Not one year has passed away, since we have been in Bristol, without more than fifty having been added to our number, each of whom, in general, needed several times to be conversed with before being admitted into fellowship. 4. That brother Craik and I have each of us the care of two churches. At the first sight it appears as if the work is thus divided, but the double number of meetings, &c., nearly double the work. 5. The mere ruling, and taking care, in general, of a large body of believers, irrespective of the other work, takes much more time, and requires much more strength, than the taking care of a small body of believers, as we, by grace, desire not to allow known sin among us. 6. The position which we have in the church at large brings many brethren to us who travel through Bristol, who call on us, or lodge with us, and to whom, according to the Lord's will, we have to give some time. 7. In my own case an extensive needful correspondence. 8. The weakness of body on the part of both of us. When the preaching is done,--when the strangers who lodge with us are gone,--when the calls at our house are over,--when the needful letters, however briefly, are written,--when the necessary church business is settled;-- our minds are often so worn out, that we are glad to be quiet. 9. But suppose we have bodily strength remaining after the above things have been attended to, yet the frame of mind is not always so, as that one could visit. After having been particularly tried by church matters, which in so large a body does not rarely occur, or being

5

cast down in one's own soul, one may be fit for the closet, but not for visiting the saints. 10. Lastly, in my own case, no small part of my time is taken up by attending to the affairs of the Orphan-Houses, Schools, the circulation of the Scriptures, the aiding Missionary efforts, and other work connected with the Scriptural Knowledge Institution.

III. What is to be done under these circumstances? 1. In the days of the Apostles there would have been more brethren to take the oversight of so large a body as we are. The Lord has not laid upon us a burden which is too heavy for us; He is not a hard master. It is evident that He does not mean us even to attempt to visit all the saints as much as is absolutely needful, and much less as frequently as it would be desirable. We mention this, to prevent uncomfortable feelings on the part of the dear saints under our pastoral care, who find themselves not as much visited as they used to be when we came to Bristol, when the number of them was not 70, and now it is about 400, and when in many other respects the work in our hands was not half so much, as it is now, and when we had much more bodily strength. 2. it is therefore evident that there are other pastors needed; not nominal pastors, but such as the Lord has called, to whom He has given a pastor's heart, and pastoral gifts. 3. Such may be raised up by the Lord from our own number, or the Lord may send them from elsewhere. 4. But in the meantime we should at least see whether there are not helpers among us. 5. As to the work itself, in order that time may be saved, it appears desirable that the two churches, Bethesda and Gideon, should be united into one, that the breaking of bread should be alternately, and that the number of weekly meetings should be reduced.

Oct. 21. A few weeks since I had rented a very large and a very cheap house for the Boys' Orphan-House; but as the persons who lived in that neighbourhood threatened the landlord with an action, on account of letting his house for a charitable institution, I, at once, gave up all claim. That which led me to do so, was the word of the Lord; "As much as lieth in you, live peaceably with all men." I was quite sure when I gave up the agreement, that the Lord would provide other premises. On the same morning when this took place, Oct. 5, the Lord, to show His continued approbation of the work, sent 50l. by a sister, who is far from being rich, for the furnishing of the Boys' Orphan-House. Now, today, the Lord has given me another house for the Orphan-Boys, in the same street, in which the other two Orphan-Houses are. Thus, in His own time, He has sent help in this particular also. Indeed in everything, in which I have had to deal with Him alone in this work, I have never been disappointed.

Oct. 23. Today two young sisters were received into fellowship who have been in our Sunday-School. Thus we begin now to reap fruit in respect of our schools.

Nov. 1. Our Bible-School and Missionary funds having been for some time very low, I had been led repeatedly to ask the Lord for a rich supply, and mentioned several times, though with submission to His will, the sum of 100l. before Him. However, He seemed not to regard the prayer respecting the 100l., but gave to us by little and little what was needed. Yesterday I received a donation of 80l., and today one of 20l., and thus He has kindly given the 100l. By this means we are able to increase our stock of Bibles, which has been much reduced of late.

Nov. 5. Last night I awoke with a great weakness in my head, which kept me a good while awake. I at last got to sleep by tying a handkerchief round my head, and by thus pressing it. Today, however, though weak, I was able to preach, and that with much enjoyment, especially in the evening at Bethesda.

Nov. 6. I feel very weak in my head. This evening it was settled at a meeting of the two churches, assembling at Bethesda and Gideon Chapels, that, for the reasons before given, the two churches should be henceforth united as one.

Nov. 7. My head is so weak, that I see it absolutely needful to give up the work for some time. After I had come this morning to the conclusion to leave Bristol for a while for the purpose of quietness, I received an anonymous letter from Ireland with 5l. for my own personal expenses, and thus the Lord has kindly supplied me with the means for doing so.--I can work no longer, my head being in such a weak stated from continual exertion, so that I feel now comfortable in going, though scarcely any time could have been, humanly speaking, more unsuitable. The Orphan-House for the Boys is on the point of being opened, the labourers therefore are to be introduced into the work;---most important church matters have been entered upon and are yet unsettled;---but the Lord knows better, and cares for His work more than I do or can. Therefore I desire to leave the matter with Him, and He graciously helps me to do so, and thus, in the quiet submission to His will, and the willingness to leave the work in His own hands, I have the testimony that I have not been engaged in my own work but in His.

Nov. 8. This morning I left Bristol. When I left my house, I knew not what place to go to. All I knew was, that I must leave Bristol. A Bath coach was the first one I could get, and I took it. My intention was, not to go to brethren, as I needed perfect quietness; but I felt so uncomfortable at the hotel, on account of the worldliness of the place, that I went to see a brother, who with his aunts kindly pressed me to stay with them.--This evening has been a very trying season to me. My head has been very weak; I have greatly feared lest I should become insane; but amidst it all, through grace, my soul is quietly resting upon the Lord.

Nov. 12. Lord's day. I am still staying in Bath. The weakness of my head allowed me to attend but one meeting, and even that distressed my head much.

Nov. 13. I was greatly distressed this evening on account of my head. I prayed earnestly to be kept from insanity.

Nov. 14. I am rather better in my head today.

Nov. 15. I left Bath, and went back to Bristol, as I felt I needed more quietness than I can have in the house of any friends, being continually drawn into conversation, which my head cannot bear.

Nov. 16. Today I went to Weston Super Mare, to take lodgings for myself and family. A sister sent me this morning 5l., by which the Lord has provided me with the means for removing my family.

Nov. 17. Weston Super Mare. This evening my wife and child, and our servant arrived here. Yesterday a sister secretly put two sovereigns in my wife's pocket book. How kind is the Lord in thus providing us with means according to our need! How kind also in having just now sent brother T. to take the work arising from the Schools, Orphan-Houses, &c., just as brother C--r was sent two years ago, shortly before I was completely laid aside!---Today a brother sent me information, that he had ordered one hundred pairs of blankets to be sent to me, for distribution among the poor.

Nov. 23. My general health is pretty good; my head, however, is no better, but rather worse. This evening I was led, through the affliction in my head, to great irritability of temper. Of late I have had afresh painfully to experience in myself two things: 1. that affliction in itself does not lead nearer to God. 2. That we may have a good deal of leisure time and yet fail in profitably improving it. Often had I wished within the last months that I might have more time. Now the Lord has given it to me, but alas! how little of it is improved for prayer. I find it a difficult thing, whilst caring for the body, not to neglect the soul. It seems to me much easier to go on altogether regardless of the body, in the service of the Lord, than to take care of the body, in the time of sickness, and not to neglect the soul, especially in an affliction like my present one, when the head allows but little reading or thinking.---What a blessed prospect to be delivered from this wretched evil nature! I can say nothing respecting this day, and this evening in particular, but that I am a wretched man.

Nov. 24. I am now quite sure that I want more than mere quiet and change of air, even medical advice. My general health seems improved through my stay at Weston, but the disease in my head is increased. I have had many distressing moments since I have been at Weston, on account of fearing that my disease may be the forerunner of insanity; yet God has in mercy sustained me, and enabled me, in some small measure, notwithstanding my great sinfulness, to realize the blessing of being in Christ, and therefore secure for ever.

Nov. 25. We returned to Bristol. I was at peace, being able to cast myself upon the Lord respecting the calamity which I feared. This evening I saw a kind physician and surgeon, who told me that the disease is either a tendency of blood to the head, or that the nerves of the head are in a disordered state. They also told me that I had not the least reason to fear insanity. How little grateful is my soul for this!

Nov. 29. I am no better. A sister sent me today 5l. also a pickled tongue, fowls, cakes, and beautiful grapes were sent to me. My cup, as to temporal mercies, runs over.---One of the Orphan children died while I was at Weston Super Mare. There is reason to believe that she died in the faith.

Nov. 30. I am not any better. I have written to my father, perhaps, for the last time. All is well, all will be well, all cannot but be well; because I am in Christ. How precious that now, in this my sickness, I have not to seek after the Lord, but have already found Him.

Dec. 1. By the mercy of God my head is somewhat relieved. My liver is in a most inactive state, which, as my kind medical attendants tell me, has created the pressure on the top of the head, and through the inactivity of the liver, the whole system having been weakened, and my mental exertions having been continued, the nerves of the head have greatly suffered in consequence.---This evening was sent to me, anonymously, from a distance, 5l. for my own present necessities. The letter was only signed F. W.---A sister, a stranger, gave to my wife 1l. Thus the Lord remembers our increased expenditure in consequence of my affliction, and sends to us accordingly.

Dec. 4. Yesterday I met with the brethren for the breaking of bread. Today I am not so well. Every time that I meet with them, the nerves of my head are excited, and I am worse afterwards. A sister from Barnstaple sent us 1l. 15s.

Dec. 8. My head is not so well as at the end of last week. I find it difficult to be in Bristol and not to exert my mind. Prayer and the reading of the Word I can bear better than any thing. May the Lord give me grace to pray more! I see as yet scarcely a single reason, so far as I myself am concerned, why the Lord should remove this affliction from me. I do not find myself more conformed to the mind of Jesus by it.

Dec. 9. Two years ago this day, I stated my intention of establishing an Orphan-House, if God should permit. What has God wrought since! 75 orphans are now under our care, and 21 more we can receive. Several more are daily expected. During the last twelvemonth the expenses have been about 740l., and the income about 840l. In addition to this, about 400l. has been expended upon the Schools, the circulation of the Scriptures, and in aiding Missionary purposes. More than 1100l. therefore we have needed during the past year, and our good Lord has supplied all, without one single person having been asked for any thing.

Dec. 12. Today the hundred pairs of blankets arrived. How kind of the Lord to give us the privilege of being instrumental in providing, in this respect, for some of the poor, both among the saints and in the world! This donation came in most seasonably, as, on inquiring into the circumstances of some of the poor, most affecting cases of distress were discovered, on account of the want of blankets. May the Lord give me grace to deny myself, in order to provide for the necessities of the poor! How much may be done even by a little self-denial! Lord, help me!--- The blankets were of a very good quality. It is a Christlike spirit in supplying the necessities of the poor, not to ask how little will do for them, but how richly may I possibly supply their need.

Dec. 14. A sister, who a short time since had given me 5l. for my own personal expenses, gave me another 5l. today. How very kind is the Lord in providing so abundantly for us, and giving us far more than we need!

Dec. 16. My head is not at all better, but rather worse. My medical attendants have today changed the medicine. But however kind and skillful they are, however nourishing the food which I take, however much I seek to refrain from over-exertion, and however much I take exercise in the air:---till Thou, my great Physician, Thou, Creator of the Universe, Lord Jesus, dost restore me, I shall be laid aside!---I have been working a little during the last fortnight, but only a little.

Dec. 17.---Lord's day. This morning I saw the 32 orphan girls, who are above seven years old, pass under my window, to go to the chapel. When I saw these dear children in their clean dresses, and their comfortable warm cloaks; and when I saw them walking orderly under the care of a sister to the chapel; I felt grateful to God that I had been made the instrument of providing for them, seeing that they are all better off, both as it regards temporal and spiritual things, than if they were at the places from whence they were taken. I felt, that, to bring about such a sight, was worth the labour not only of many days, but of many months, or years. I felt that it answered all the arguments of some of my friends who say "you do too much."

Dec. 24. This is the seventh Lord's day that I have been laid aside.---This day I determine, by the help of God, no more to send letters in parcels, because I now clearly see that it is against the laws of the country, and it becomes me, as a disciple of Jesus, in every respect to submit myself to the Government, in so far as I am not called upon to do any thing contrary to the word of God.

Dec. 26. Today the same brother who sent me the hundred pairs of blankets, sent me 100l. to purchase as many more blankets as I can satisfactorily distribute.

Dec. 29. Applications for the admission of orphans become more and more numerous. Almost daily fresh cases are brought before us. There are already as many applications for Orphan-Girls above seven years as would fill another house. There are also many more Infant-Orphans applied for than we can take in. Truly this is a large field of labour!

Dec. 31. This is the eighth Lord's day since I have been kept from ministering in the Word, nor did I think it well, on account of my head, to go to any of the meetings today. Whether I am really getting better I know not, yet I hope I am. My head is yet much affected, though my liver seems somewhat more active.---This morning I greatly dishonoured the Lord by irritability, manifested towards my dear wife, and that almost immediately after I had been on my knees before God, praising Him for having given me such a wife.

REVIEW OF THE YEAR 1837.

I. There are now 81 children in the three Orphan-Houses, and nine brethren and sisters who have the care of them. Ninety, therefore, daily sit down to table. Lord look on the necessities of Thy servant!

II. The schools require as much help as before; nay, more, particularly the Sunday School, in which there are at present about 320 children, and in the Day Schools about 350.---Lord, Thy servant is a poor man; but he has trusted in Thee, and made his boast in Thee, before the sons of men; therefore let him not be confounded! Let it not be said, all this is enthusiasm, and therefore it is come to nought.

III. My temporal supplies have been:---

1. By the Freewill Offerings through the boxes L149 18s. 6 1/2d.

2. By Presents in money, from believers in and out of Bristol L77 4s. 0d.

3. By Presents in clothes, provisions, &c., which were worth to us at least L25 0s. 0d.

4. By Money through family connexion L45 0s. 0d.

5. We have been living half free of rent, whereby we have saved at least L10 0s. 0d.

Altogether L307 2s. 6 1/2d.

I have purposely given here again, as at the close of the former years, a statement of the supplies which the Lord has been pleased to send me during this year, because I delight in showing, both to the world and to the church, how kind a Master I have served even as to temporal blessings, and how so plainly in my ease the Lord has displayed the truth of that word "Whosoever believeth on Him shall not be confounded," not merely by providing the means for His work in my hands, but also by providing for the necessities of myself and family.

January 1, 1838. Through the good hand of our God upon me, I have been brought to the beginning of an other year. May He in mercy grant that it may be spent more in His service than any previous year! May I, through the indwelling of the Holy Spirit, be more conformed to the image of His Son, than has been the case hitherto!---Last night the brethren had a prayer meeting at Gideon, after the preaching was over, and continued till half-past twelve in prayer; but I was unable to be present.

Jan. 2. During the last night thieves broke into our house, and into the school-room of Gideon Chapel. Being stopped by a second strong door, in my house, or rather being prevented from going any further by our loving Father, who did not allow the hedge which He has set round about us, at this time, to be broken through, nothing was missing, except some cold meat, which they took out of the house.--- They broke open several boxes in Gideon school-room, but took nothing. They left some of the bones, the meat being cut off, in one of the boxes in Gideon school-room, and hung up another in a tree in our garden. So depraved is man naturally when left to himself, that he not only steals his fellowman's property, but also makes sport of the sin! How merciful that God has protected us! My mind was peaceful when I heard the news this morning, thanking God from my heart for preservation, and considering it as an answer to prayer, which had been many times put up to Him, during these last years, respecting thieves.

Jan. 6. I feel very little better in my head, though my general health seems improved; but my kind physician says I am much better, and advises me now change of air. I am most reluctant to go, though on two former occasions when I used change of air, in August 1829 at Exmouth, and in 1835 at Niton in the Isle of Wight, the Lord abundantly blessed me in doing so, both bodily and spiritually. This evening a sister who resides about fifty miles from hence, and who is therefore quite 'unacquainted with the medical advice given to me this morning, sent me 15l. for the express purpose of change of air, and wrote that she felt assured, from having been similarly afflicted, that nothing would do me so much good, humanly speaking, as quiet and change of air. How wonderfully does God work! I have thus the means of carrying into effect my physician's advice.---Today I heard of a most remarkable case of conversion through the instrumentality of my Narrative.

Jan. 7. This is the ninth Lord's day that I have been kept from ministering in the Word. My head is in a distressing state, and, as far as I can judge, as bad as ever. It seems to me more and more clear that the nerves are affected. My affliction is connected with a great tendency to irritability of temper; yea, with some satanic feeling, foreign to me even naturally. O Lord, mercifully keep Thy servant from openly dishonouring Thy name! Rather take me soon home to Thyself!

Jan. 10. Today I went with my family to Trowbridge.

Jan. 12. Trowbridge. This evening I commenced reading Whitfield's life, written by Mr. Philip.

Jan. 13. I have already received blessings through Whitfield's life. His great success in preaching the Gospel is evidently to be ascribed, instrumentally, to his great prayerfulness, and his reading the Bible on his knees. I have known the importance of this for years; I have practiced it a little, but far too little. I have had more communion with God today than I have had, at least generally, for some time past.

Jan. 14. Lord's day. I have, continued reading Whitfield's life. God has again blessed it to my soul. I have spent several hours in prayer today, and read on my knees, and prayed for two hours over Psalm lxiii. God has blessed my soul much today. I have been fighting together with the armies of Jesus, though this is the tenth Lord's day since I have been kept from preaching, and though I have not assembled with the brethren here, on account of my head. My soul is now brought into that state, that I delight myself in the will of God, as it regards my health. Yea, I can now say, from my heart, I would not have this disease removed till God, through it, has bestowed the blessing for which it was sent. He has drawn out my soul much yesterday and today. Lord, continue Thy goodness, and fill me with love! I long, more fully to glorify God; not so much by outward activity, as by inward conformity to the image of Jesus. What hinders God, to make of one, so vile as I am, another Whitfield? Surely, God could bestow as much grace upon me, as He did upon him. O, my Lord, draw me closer and closer to Thyself, that I may run after Thee!--- I desire, if God should restore me again for the ministry of the Word (and this I believe He will do soon, judging from the state in which He has now brought my soul, though I have been worse in health the last eight days, than for several weeks previously), that my preaching may be more than ever the result of earnest prayer and much meditation, and that I may so walk with God, that "out of my belly may flow rivers of living water." But alas! if the grace of God prevent not, one day more, and the rich blessings, which He has bestowed upon my soul yesterday and today, will all vanish; but again, if He favours me (and oh! may He do it), I shall go from strength to strength, and I and the saints in Bristol shall have abundant reason to praise God for this my illness.

Jan. 15. I have had since yesterday afternoon less suffering in my head than for the last eight days! though it is even now far from being well. I have still an inward assurance, on account of the spiritual blessings which the Lord has granted to me, that through this affliction He is only purifying me for His blessed service, and that I shall be soon restored to the work.---Today, also, God has continued to me fervency of spirit, which I have now enjoyed for three days following. He has today, also, drawn out my soul into much real communion with Himself, and into holy desires to be more conformed to His dear Son. When God gives a spirit of prayer, how easy then to pray! Nevertheless it was given to me in the use of the means, as I fell on my knees last Saturday, to read His Word with meditation, and to turn it into prayer. Today I spent about three hours in prayer over Ps. lxiv. and lxv. In reference to that precious word! "O thou that hearest prayer," (Ps. lxv. 2.) I asked the Lord the following petitions, and entreated Him to record them in heaven and to answer them.

1. That He would give me grace to glorify Him by a submissive and patient spirit under my affliction.

2. That, as I was enabled now, and only now from my heart, to praise God for this affliction, He would not remove His hand from me, until He had qualified me for His work more than I have been hitherto.

3. That He would be pleased to grant, that the work of conversion, through the instrumentality of brother Craik and myself, might not cease, but go on as much now as when we first came to Bristol, yea, more abundantly than even then.

4. That He would be pleased to give more real spiritual prosperity to the church under our care, than ever we have as yet enjoyed.

5. Having praised Him for the sale of so many copies of my Narrative in so short a time, I entreated Him to cause every copy to be disposed of.

6. I asked Him to continue to let His rich blessing rest upon this little work, and more abundantly, so that many may be converted through it, and many of the children of God truly benefited by it; and that thus I might now be speaking through it, though laid aside from active service.

7. I asked Him for His blessing, in the way of conversion, to rest upon the Orphans, and upon the Sunday and Day-School children under our care.

8. I asked Him for means to carry on these Institutions, and to enlarge them.

These are some of the petitions which I have asked of my God this evening in connexion with this His own word. I believe He has heard me. I believe He will make it manifest, in His own good time, that He has heard me; and I have recorded these my petitions this 14th day of January, 1838, that, when God has answered them, He may get, through this, glory to His name.---[Whilst writing this second part, I add to the praise of the Lord, and for the encouragement of the children of God, that petitions 4, 5, 6, 7, and 8, have been fully answered, and the other petitions, likewise, in part.]

Jan. 16, Tuesday. A blessed day. How very good is the Lord! Fervency of spirit, through His grace, is continued to me, though this morning, but for the help of God, I should have lost it again. The weather has been very cold for several days; but today

I suffered much, either because it was colder than before, or because I felt it more, owing to the weakness of my body, and having taken so much medicine. I arose from my knees, and stirred the fire; but I still remained very cold. I was a little irritated by this. I moved to another part of the room, but felt the cold still more. At last, having prayed for some time, I was obliged to rise up, and take a walk to promote circulation. I now entreated the Lord on my walk, that this circumstance might not be permitted to rob me of the precious communion which I have had with Him the last three days; for this was the object at which Satan aimed. I confessed also my sin of irritability on account of the cold, and sought to have my conscience cleansed through the blood of Jesus. He had mercy upon me, my peace was restored; and when I returned I sought the Lord again in prayer, and had uninterrupted communion with Him. [I have purposely mentioned the above circumstance, in detail, in order to show, how the most trivial causes may operate in suddenly robbing one of the enjoyment of most blessed communion with God.] I have been enabled to pray for several hours this day. The subject of my meditation has been Psalm lxvi.--Verses 10, 11, and 12, are particularly applicable to my present circumstances. God has already, through the instrumentality of this my affliction, brought me into a "wealthy place," and I believe He will bless my soul yet more and more.---I do not remember any time, when I have had more fervency of spirit in connexion with such a desire to overcome every thing that is hateful in the sight of God, and with such an earnestness to be fully conformed to the image of Jesus. Truly, I have reason to apply to myself verse 16, and "tell what God has done for my soul."--Verse 18 also I can take to myself. I do not regard iniquity in my heart, but it is upright before Him, through His grace, and therefore God does hear my prayers.--What has God done for me, in comparing this 16th of January 1838 with the 16th of January 1820, the day on which my dear mother died.--I have also resolved this day, if the Lord should restore me again, to have an especial meeting at the chapel once a week, or once a fortnight, with the Orphan and Day-School children, for the purpose of reading the Scriptures with them.---My heart has been drawn out in prayer for many things, especially that the Lord would create in me a holy earnestness to win souls, and a greater compassion for ruined sinners. For this I have been quickened through reading onward in Whitfield's life.

Jan. 17. The Lord is yet merciful to me. I enjoy fervency of spirit. My soul has been again repeatedly led out in prayer this day, and that for a considerable time.-- I have read on my knees, with prayer and meditation, Psalm lxviii.--Verse 5 "A Father of the fatherless," one of the titles of Jehovah, has been an especial blessing to me, with reference to the Orphans. The truth, which is contained in this, I never realized so much as today. By the help of God, this shall be my argument before Him, respecting the Orphans, in the hour of need. He is their Father, and therefore has pledged Himself, as it were, to provide for them, and to care for them; and I have only to remind Him of the need of these poor children, in order to have it supplied. My soul is still more enlarged respecting Orphans. This word "a Father of the fatherless," contains enough encouragement to cast thousands of Orphans, with all their need, upon the loving heart of God.--My head has been again in a distressing state today; my soul, however, is in peace. May God in mercy continue to me fervency of spirit!

January 18 to February 2. During this time I continued still at Trowbridge. I was, on the whole, very happy, and habitually at peace, and had repeatedly much communion with God; but still I had not the same earnestness in prayer, nor did I, in other respects, enjoy the same degree of fervency of spirit, with which the Lord had favoured me for several days previous to this period. While the considerable degree of fervency of spirit, which I had had, was altogether the gift of God, still I have to ascribe to myself the loss of it. It is remarkable, that the same book, Whitfield's Life, which was instrumental in stirring me up to seek after such a frame of heart, was also instrumental in depriving me of it, in some measure, afterwards. I once or twice read that book when I ought to have read the Bible on my knees, and thus was robbed of a blessing. Nevertheless, on the whole, even this period was a good season.--My health being not at all improved, it seemed best that I should give up all medicine for a while, and take a tour; on which account I left Trowbridge today and went to Bath, with the object of going from thence to Oxford. I had grace today to confess the Lord Jesus on my way from Trowbridge to Bath, as also twice, lately, in going from Trowbridge to Bristol; but I was also twice silent. Oh that my heart may be filled with the love of Jesus, in order that it maybe filled with love for perishing sinners!

Feb. 3. I left Bath this morning, and arrived in the evening at Oxford, where I was very kindly received by brother and sister ----, and the sisters ----.

Feb. 7. Oxford. I had been praying repeatedly yesterday and the day before, that the Lord would be pleased to guide me, whether I should leave this place or not; but could not see it clearly to be His will that I should do so, and therefore determined to stay. Now, as I am able to have a quiet horse, I shall try horse exercise, if it may please the Lord to bless that to the benefit of my health.

Feb. 10. I have had horse exercise for the last three days, but the horse is now ill. "Mine hour is not yet come," is the Lord's voice to me in this little circumstance.

Feb. 11. This morning I was directed to read Proverbs iii. 5-12, having just a few minutes to fill up before breakfast. I was particularly struck with those words: "Neither be weary of His correction." I have not been allowed to despise the chastening of the Lord, but I begin, now and then, to feel somewhat weary of His correction. O Lord, have mercy upon Thy poor unworthy servant! Thou knowest, that, after the inner man, I desire patiently to bear this affliction, and not to have it removed till it has done its work in me, and yielded the peaceable fruits of righteousness. But Thou knowest also what a trial it is to me to continue the life I am now living. Help, Lord, according to my need!

On Feb. 8th I sent a letter to the church in Bristol, which, having been preserved, I give here in print, as it shows the way in which the Lord dealt with me during and through the instrumentality of the affliction, and which, with His blessing, may lead one or other of the children of God who are in trial, quietly to wait for the end, and to look out for blessings to be bestowed upon them through the instrumentality of the trial.

To the Saints, united together in Fellowship, and assembling at Bethesda and Gideon Chapels, Bristol.

Trowbridge, Feb. 1, 1838.

Dear Brethren,

Twelve weeks have passed away, since I last ministered among you. I should have written to you repeatedly, during that period, had I not thought it better to put aside every mental occupation which could be deferred, as my head is unfit for mental exertion; but I would now rather write a few lines, than appear unmindful of you. You are dear to me; yea, so dear, that I desire to live and die with you, if our Lord permit; and why should I not tell you so by letter? I will write, then, as a token of brotherly remembrance and of love towards you; and may it be a means of quickening you to prayer on my behalf.

In looking back upon my past life, I know not where to begin, and where to end, in making mention of the Lord's mercies. His long-suffering towards me in the days of my unregeneracy cannot be described. You know a little of my sinful life, before I was brought to the Lord; still you know but very little. If, however, I have much reason to praise God for His mercies towards me in those days, I have more abundant reason to admire His gentleness, long-suffering, and faithfulness towards me since I have known Him. He has step by step led me on, and He has not broken the bruised reed. His gentleness towards me has been great indeed, very great. (Brethren, let us follow God, in dealing gently with each other!) He has borne with my coldness, half-heartedness, and backsliding. In the midst of it all, He has treated me as His child. How can I sufficiently praise Him for this long-suffering? (Brethren, let us imitate our Father, let us bear long, and suffer long with each other!) He has been always the same gracious, kind, loving Father, Friend, Supporter, Teacher, Comforter, and all in all to me, as He was at the beginning. No variableness has been found in Him towards me, though I have again and again provoked Him. I say this to my shame. (Brethren, let us seek to be faithful, in the Lord, towards each other! Let us seek to love each other in the truth, and for the truth's sake, without variableness! It is easy, comparatively, to begin to love; but it requires much watchfulness, not to grow weary in love, when little or no love is returned; yea, when we are unkindly treated, instead of being loved. But as our gracious, faithful God, notwithstanding all our

17

variableness, loves us without change, so should we, His children, love each other. Lord, help us so to do!)

Besides this gentleness, long-suffering, and faithfulness, which the Lord has manifested towards me, and which I have experienced in common with you all, the Lord has bestowed upon me peculiar blessings and privileges. One of the chief is, that He has condescended to call me for the ministry of His word. How can I praise Him sufficiently for this! One who was such a sinner, such a servant of Satan, so fit for hell, so deserving of everlasting destruction, was not merely cleansed from sin and made a child of God through faith in the Lord Jesus, and thus fitted for heaven, and did not merely receive the sure promise that he should have eternal glory; but was also called unto, and, in a measure, qualified for the expounding of the word of God. I magnify Him for this honour!---But more than this. More than eleven years, with very little interruption, have I been allowed, more or less, to preach the Word. My soul does magnify the Lord for this! More still. The Lord has condescended to use me as an instrument in converting many sinners, and, in a measure at least, in benefiting many of His children. For this honour I do now praise God, and shall praise Him not merely as long as I live, but as long as I have a being. But I do not stop here. I have many other reasons to speak well of the Lord, but I would only mention one. It is my present affliction. Yes, my present affliction is among the many things, for which I have very much reason to praise God; and I do praise Him for it. Before you, before the whole church of Christ, and before the world would I confess that God has dealt in very kindness towards me in this affliction. I own, I have not borne it without impatience and fretfulness; I own, I have been several times overcome by irritability of temper on account of it; but nevertheless, after the inner man, I praise God for the affliction, and I do desire from my heart, that it may truly benefit me, and that it may not be removed till the end has been answered, for which it has been sent. God has blessed me in this trial, and is still blessing me.-- As I know you love me, (unworthy as I am of it), and feel interested about me, I mention a few of the many mercies with which God has favoured me during these twelve weeks. 1. At the commencement of my illness, when my head was affected in a manner quite new to me, and when thus it continued day after day, I feared lest I should lose my reason.--This created more real internal suffering than ever I had known before. But our gracious Lord supported me. His precious gospel was full of comfort to me. All, all will be well, was invariably the conclusion, the conclusion grounded upon Scripture, to which I came; yea, all will be well with me eternally, though the heaviest of all earthly trials should coins upon me, even that of dying in a state of insanity.--I was once near death, as I then thought, nearly nine years ago: I was full of comfort at that time; but to be comfortable,--to be able quietly to repose upon God, with the prospect of an affliction before one, such as I have now mentioned,--is more than to be comfortable in the prospect of death, at least for a believer.--Now, is it not well to be afflicted, in order to obtain such an experience? And have I not reason, therefore, to thank God for this affliction?

Oxford, Feb. 6, 1838.

When I began to write the foregoing lines, beloved brethren, I intended to write but very briefly; but as I love you, and as I have abundant reason to magnify the Lord, my pen ran on, till my head would follow no longer.--I go on now to mention some other mercies which the Lord has bestowed upon me, through my present affliction.

2. Through being deprived for so long a time of the privilege of preaching the Word to sinners and saints, the Lord has been pleased to create in me a longing for this blessed work, and to give me at the same time to feel the importance of it, in a degree in which I never had experienced it before. Thus the Lord has fitted me somewhat more for His work, by laying me aside from it. Good therefore is the Lord, and kind indeed, in disabling me from preaching. Great has been my trial, after the self-willed old nature, not to be able to preach; and long ere this, unfit as I was for it, I should have resumed the work, had I followed my own will; but hitherto have I considered it most for the glory of God, quietly to refrain from outward service, in order to glorify Him by patient submission, till my Lord shall be pleased to condescend to call His servant forth again for active engagements. And then, I know, He will give me grace, cheerfully to go back to the delightful service of pointing sinners to the Lamb of God, and of feeding the church.

3. Through this affliction I have known experimentally in a higher degree than I knew it before, how, if obliged to refrain from active service, one can nevertheless as really and truly help the armies of Jesus, through secret prayer, as if one were actively engaged in the proclamation of the truth.--This point brings to my mind a truth, of which we all need to be reminded frequently, even this, that at all times, and under all circumstances, we may really and truly serve the Lord, and fight for His kingdom, by seeking to manifest His mind, and by giving ourselves to prayer.

4. Through the instrumentality of this affliction the Lord has been pleased to show me, how I may lay out myself more fully for His service in the proclamation of His truth; and, by His grace, if ever restored for active service, I purpose to practice what He has shown me.

5. Through being deprived so much from meeting with the brethren as I have been these thirteen weeks, I have learned somewhat more to value this privilege than I did before. For as my head has been much affected, even through one meeting on the Lord's day, I have seen how highly I ought to have prized the days, when twice or thrice I could meet with the saints, without suffering from it.--Bear with me, brethren, when I beseech you, highly to esteem the opportunities of assembling yourselves together. Precede them with prayer; for only in as much as you do so, have you a right to expect a blessing from them. Seek to treasure up, not merely in your memory, but in your heart, the truths which you hear; for soon you may be deprived of these privileges, and soon you may be called upon to practice what you

hear. Brethren, let us not learn the greatness of our privileges, by being deprived of them.--

I also delight in mentioning some of the particulars in which the Lord's kindness to me has appeared in this affliction, and whereby He has shown, that He does not lay more on us, than is absolutely needful.

1. You know, that since May, 1836, I was able to walk but little. This infirmity the Lord entirely removed, just before I became afflicted in my head. This was exceedingly kind; for air and exercise are the only means, which almost immediately relieve my head. How much greater would have been the affliction, had I not been able to walk about in the air!---Truly, "He stayeth His rough wind, in the day of His east wind." I delight in pointing out the gentleness of the stroke.

Oxford, Feb. 7, 1838.

2. The Lord might have chosen to confine me to my bed, and kept me there in much pain these thirteen weeks, for the sake of teaching me the lessons which He purposes me to learn through this affliction; instead of this, the pain in my head has been so slight, that it would not be worth mentioning, were it not connected with a weakness of the mental faculties, which allows of but little exertion.

3. Further, it might have pleased the Lord to incapacitate me altogether for active service, but instead of this, He has still allowed me, in some small measure, to help by my judgment in some church matters, to write some letters in His service, to speak now and then a word to believers for the furtherance of their faith, and to confess His name repeatedly before unconverted persons, with whom I have met on my journeys. Besides all this, I have had strength for other work connected with the kingdom of Jesus Christ.

4. In one other point the Lord has been especially gracious to me, in that, while I have been unable to preach, unable to write or read much, or even to converse for any length of time with the brethren, He has allowed me always sufficient strength for as much secret prayer as I desired. Even praying with others has been often trying to my head; but prayer in secret has not only never tried my head, but has been habitually (I mean the act of prayer) a relief to my head. Oh! how can I sufficiently praise God for this. How comparatively slight are any trials to a child of God, as long as under them he is enabled to converse freely with his Father! And so sweet has been this communion with my Father, a few times, and so have I been enabled to pour out my heart before Him, that whilst those favoured seasons have lasted, I not only felt the affliction to be no affliction, and could call it, from my heart, sweet affliction; but I was almost unwilling soon to go back to the multiplicity of engagements in Bristol, lest I should not have leisure to continue so much in prayer, meditation, and the study of His word. Shall I not then praise my Father for such

dealings with me? Do I not even now see this affliction working for my good? I say, therefore, after the inward man: Father, continue Thy hand upon me, as long as it shall seem good in Thy sight, only bless my soul!---But, brethren, do not mistake me, as if I meant that I prayed habitually with much earnestness. O no! I pray a little habitually, I pray now and then much; but I pray by no means as much as my strength and present time allow me. Therefore ask God on my behalf, that grace may be given me, habitually to pray much; and you will surely be profited by it.--But I could not help alluding to this point, as the Lord's kindness is so particularly seen in this matter.

5. Lastly, I cannot omit mentioning the kindness of the Lord, in opening the houses of some of His children at Bath, Trowbridge, and Oxford for me, during this my affliction. These dear saints have shown me much kindness. But while I would be grateful to them for it, I discern the hand of God in influencing their hearts. Moreover, I have had kind medical attendants. And you, my dear brethren, though I have been unable to minister among you, have continued to supply my temporal wants, for which I thank you, and in all of which I see the gracious, loving hand of my Father, who through all this, as by a voice from heaven, tells me: "My child, even bodily health and strength would I give, were it good for thee." I therefore desire to wait for the good pleasure of my God concerning this point.

Your love will naturally ask, how I now am in body. My disease, as my kind medical friends tell me, is an inactive liver, which causes the pain in the head, and the inability of exerting my mind for any length of time. In addition to this, the nerves of the head seem to have suffered through over-exertion. As medicine had been tried for about ten weeks, and had not given relief, it appeared well, that I should give it up for a time, and simply travel about for the benefit of the air. My own experience teaches me, that this means is beneficial; for it gives almost immediate relief. In consequence of this, I left Trowbridge last Friday, and arrived on Saturday evening at Oxford, where I am staying with dear brother and sister B. I have here all that brotherly love can do for me, and am in every way comfortable. It is now a week since I have given up medicine, and I am at least not worse, if not better; but I think I am a little better. I wait on the Lord to show me His will, as to the place to which I should go next.

As to my inner man, I am in peace, generally in peace, and long for more conformity to the mind of Christ. My chief desire is, that if it shall ever please the Lord to restore me again, to be sent back to active service with increased humility, greater earnestness in the work, greater love for perishing sinners, and a heart habitually influenced by the truths which I preach.--Whether I shall ever be restored for the work, I cannot say with certainty; but, if I may judge from the Lord's dealings with me in former times, I have reason to believe, that I shall yet be allowed to labour again.

In conclusion, dear brethren, pray for my dear brother and fellow-labourer. Esteem him highly in the Lord; for He is worthy of all honour.---I would write more, for I have much more to speak of; but as I purpose, if God allows me the pleasure, to write again soon, I leave it till then. Farewell.

Your affectionate brother and servant in the Lord,

GEORGE MULLER.

Feb. 13. These ten days I have been staying in Oxford, though I came only for one or two; but I have stayed to see the Lord's hand leading me away from hence. I have now been led to decide on going to Lutterworth to see brother---, to converse with him about accompanying him on a journey to the Continent, with reference to Missionary objects. When I had come to this decision, I took another ride, the horse being well again; but now this formerly quiet horse was self-willed and shy, which does not at all suit me in the weak state of my nervous system. As horse exercise had kept me here longer than I had intended to stay, and as I cannot now ride on this horse which before suited me so well, I see, even in this, in itself, trifling circumstance, a confirmation that I had been right in my decision to leave Oxford.

Feb. 16. Lutterworth. I arrived here on the evening of the 14th. I have been decidedly worse since I have been here, and was obliged again to have recourse to medicine. A brother having strongly recommended me, whilst in Oxford, to go to Leamington on account of my health, and having at the same time offered to pay my expenses during my stay there, and being now so very unwell again, and so near Leamington, I decided to-night upon accepting his kindness, provided that my kind physician in Bristol had no objection.

Feb. 17. Leamington. I left Lutterworth this morning, where I have received much kindness. There was no inside place, and I was very unwell; but the fear of being quite laid up at Lutterworth, and becoming burthensome to those dear saints who had received me into their house though a stranger to them; and having still no desirable medical advice; and the remembrance that the Lord had graciously enabled me, even lately, to travel outside in cold weather; induced me to get on the coach, and I rode off in a heavy fall of snow. But God had mercy. After eight miles ride, at Rugby, I obtained an inside place. The rest of the way was crowned with mercies. I had a room to myself at Southam, found a suitable dinner just ready, had an inside place to Leamington, and was preserved by the way, though the coachman was quite intoxicated, and drove furiously.--I had asked the Lord to let me find a suitable and cheap lodging at Leamington, and the first lodging I saw I took, for which I pay only ten shillings weekly. Thus, a few minutes after my arrival, I sat comfortably at my own fireside. How very kind of the Lord!

Feb. 26. Yesterday and today I have suffered again in my head, though I have been on the whole better since I have taken the Leamington waters. But far more trying has been the internal conflict which I have had. Grace fought against evil suggestions of one kind and another, and prevailed; but it was a very trying season. This was much increased by receiving neither yesterday nor today a letter from my dear wife. Grace sought out for reasons why she had not written; nevertheless it was a very trying season. Today I earnestly prayed to God to send my wife to me, as I feel that by being alone, and afflicted as I am in my bead, and thus fit for little mental employment, Satan gets an advantage over me.

Feb. 27. God has had mercy upon me. The sore and sharp trial, the very bitter conflict is over.--This morning also I received a letter, which ought to have come yesterday, and which showed me that my dear wife had not been remiss in writing. She announced her purpose of coming today, and God, in mercy to me, brought her safely.

March 3. My head has been on the whole better these two weeks, than it has been for several months; but still I am not well. I have walked every day, for the last thirteen days, between three and four hours a day, and by the mercy of God am able to do so, without much fatigue.

March 11. My health is much the same. I am pretty well, but have no mental energy.--I have read during the last weeks once more, with as much or more interest than ever, I. and II. of Samuel, and I. and II. of Kings.---I have now, after repeated prayer, come to the conclusion, (if brother Craik, to whom I have written, sees no objection, and if my physician thinks it would be beneficial to my health,) to accompany brother--to Germany, that thus; 1, I might aid him by my advice in reference to the object of his journey; 2, that thus, if the Lord will, through the journey and the benefit of my native air, my health might be benefited; and 3, that I might once more have an opportunity of setting the truth before my father and brother.

March 12. I feel quite comfortable in the prospect of going to Germany. I trust it will prove to be as much of God, as it was shown to have been the last time.

March 13. I had a letter today from brother Craik, who thinks it desirable that I should go to Germany, but my physician says that I should not go for a month or two, for that my mind ought not to be burdened. I am in peace, and from this I see that the Lord has made me willing to do His and not my own will. I wrote to brother----the result of today, and have now left it with him, whether he will wait, or go on the 21st, as he purposes.

March 14--20. During these days, as before, I have continued to read the Scriptures with prayer, i. e. turning what I read into prayer, chiefly with a reference to myself. My days generally pass away in peace. It is a trial to me, to have to care so much about my body; but, on the whole, the Lord gives me grace to submit patiently, yet not always. Today I saw again my medical adviser, who wishes me to stay another week.

March 23, Today I received a letter from brother ----. He is not gone, and will wait for me. I have increased assurance that I shall go to Berlin, and have comfort in the thought.

March 24. A few days ago I had particular comfort in meditating on the Lord's prayer in Luke (which came in the course of my meditation), after having been tempted to pass it over, as it had been the subject of my meditation a short time before.--Within the last fortnight I have read with meditation and prayer from the 4th to the 12th chapter of the Gospel by Luke.

April 2. For some time I have been getting weary of my stay here. Yesterday I pleaded especially that word Psalm ciii. 13: "Like as a father pitieth his children, so the Lord pitieth them that fear Him." I begged God to pity me, and to release me from the necessity of staying any longer at Leamington, if it might be. Today I saw my physician, and he has allowed me to leave. Thus the Lord has granted my request.

April 3. My dear Mary left for Bristol, and I for London, on my way to Germany. I was led to read, this morning, Psalm cxxi. with my dear wife before we separated, which we both felt to be very appropriate to our circumstances.

April 6. This evening I went on board the steamer for Hamburg.

April 7. All the day ill from sea sickness.

April 8. Lord's day. I was able to get up this morning, and to take my meals.--Last night I was led to praise God for having made me His child, considering that I was most likely the only one on board that knew Him. This morning, however, I found a sister in the Lord among the passengers, with whom I had much conversation.--At dinner she manifested more grace, in testifying against evil, than I did. At tea time I had grace, in some measure, to speak of Jesus before the company, and to confess Him as my Lord.

April 9. We arrived at Hamburg about one in the morning, having had a most favourable passage of about 48 hours, and at seven I went on shore. It had been repeatedly my prayer, that I might soon find out brother ----, who had gone three days before me to Hamburg; and immediately after my arrival, in answer to prayer, without any difficulty, I found out where he lodged.

April 14. Berlin. We arrived here the evening before last. Having been yesterday and this morning seeking for lodgings, without being able to obtain any that were suitable, I at last became irritated. Surely there was lack of earnest prayer on my part in this matter, and want of patience in waiting the Lord's own time, and want of openness, in not telling brother ---- that I was tired, and that, on account of my weakness, I was unable thus to go about from place to place. At last the Lord directed us to two suitable rooms, and I feel now again comfortable, in my quiet retirement, after having confessed my sin of irritability to the Lord and to brother ----.

April 15--21. We met several times during this week with certain brethren who desire to give themselves to Missionary service, and prayed and read the Scriptures with them, and made such remarks as seemed to be important in connexion with the work. In addition to this we saw the brethren privately at our lodgings, two, three, or four at a time. But I have still felt the great weakness of my mental powers, and have been only able to attend to this work about three hours a day.--Since my arrival here I have had two letters from my dear Mary. Harriet Culliford, one of the Orphans, and formerly one of the most unpromising children, has been removed. She died as a true believer, several of the brethren who saw her being quite satisfied about her state. Surely this pays for much trouble and for much expense! My wife also mentions some fresh instances of the Lord's blessing resting upon my Narrative.--I am now, after prayer, this day, April 21, quite sure that I should leave Berlin, and go to my father at once, as the work here is too much for my head.

April 22nd. Confirmation-day of the children in Berlin. The son of the person with whom we lodge was confirmed, and in the evening they had the violin and dancing. How awful!---A few days since I heard that a brother in the Lord, an old friend of mine, and one of the two alluded to in the first part of this Narrative, page 15, was in prison on account of his religious views. This brought afresh before me the privileges which the children of God enjoy in England.--I saw a few days since another brother in prison, who, as an unconverted young man, in the university, was once at a political club, and had his name enrolled, in consequence of this, in the list of the political students. Shortly afterwards he was converted, and gave up all connexion with these political students. He finished his university course and afterwards became a tutor to the sons of a baron. In that family he had been for a considerable time, when one night he was fetched by the police out of his bed and taken to prison, on the ground of this his connexion with the political club three or four years before. [The result was that he was for many months in prison. Now he is a Missionary in the East Indies. I have related this circumstance to remind the reader afresh, that though the Lord freely and fully forgives us all our sins at once when we believe, yet He may allow us to suffer the consequences of them in a greater or less degree.]

April 24. Left Berlin last evening for Magdeburg, Had a long conversation with two deists in the mail. God helped me to make a full confession of His dear Son, in answer to prayer for grace to be enabled to do so. This afternoon I arrived at Heimersleben, the small town where my father lives. Once more then I have met with my dear aged parent, who is evidently fast hastening to the grave, and seems to me not likely to live through the next winter. I arrived just at the time when, the Fair was held in the town. How great, how exceedingly great, the difference in me, as to my feelings respecting such things now, from what they were formerly!

April 25--28. Stay at Heimersleben. The Lord has given me both an opportunity and grace to speak more fully, more simply, and more to the heart of my father about the things of God, and in particular about the plan of salvation, than I had ever done before. I trust that, in judgment at least, he is convinced that there is something lacking in him. All the time of my stay here he has been most affectionate. I spoke also fully again to my poor brother, who is now completely living in open sin. Oh to grace what a debtor am I!---Brother Knabe, who was the only believer in Heimersleben, as far as I have been able to learn, died about eighteen months since.

April 28. Today I left for Magdeburg. My father accompanied me about eight miles. Both of us, I think, felt, when about to separate, that we were parting from each other, never again to meet on earth. How would it have cheered the separation on both sides, were my dear father a believer! But it made my heart indeed sad to see him, in all human probability, for the last time, without having Scriptural ground for hope respecting his soul.--I arrived in the afternoon at Magdeburg, and went to a brother, a musician in one of the regiments of that fortress, who is on the point of leaving the army to go to the East Indies as a Missionary. In his lodgings I saw another brother, a private soldier, who lives in the barracks, who told me, on my enquiring, that he goes into the sand cellar, which is perfectly dark, in order to obtain opportunity for secret prayer. How great the privileges of those who may freely have both time and place for retirement; but how great, at the same time, our obligation to improve these opportunities!---This evening at eight I went on board an Elbe-steamer for Hamburg.

April 30. This morning at seven I arrived at Hamburg. Nothing particular happened during the passage, except that we stuck fast, in a shallow part of the river, through the carelessness of one of the sailors; but the Lord heard prayer, and after a little while the steamer could ply again.

May 1. Yesterday and today I spent in an hotel at Hamburg in writing letters. I had also, though staying at an hotel, much real communion with God in reading the Scriptures and in prayer. This evening I embarked for London.

May 4. London. Left Hamburg on the 2nd. Had a fine passage. I have, by the mercy of God, been kept from light and trifling conversation; but I have not confessed the Lord Jesus as plainly as I ought to have done. This afternoon I arrived at the house of my dear friends in London, who received me with their usual kindness. After prayer I see it my duty to leave tomorrow for Leamington, to see my physician there once more, and then to go as soon as I can to Bristol.

May 5. Leamington. Through the mercy of the Lord the journey to Germany, concerning which I had prayed so often, is now over, and I am safely brought back again to this place.--It has been a wet and cold day, but God has in mercy preserved me from injury, though I got wet. I had some conversation with a clergyman on the coach; I confessed the Lord Christ a little, but not plainly enough.--I had asked the Lord to give me a quiet and cheap resting place in my former lodgings, if it might be, and accordingly they were unlet.

May 7. This morning I left Leamington for Bristol. I had grace to confess the Lord Jesus the last part of the way before several merry passengers, and had the honour of being ridiculed for His sake. There are few things in which I feel more entirely dependant upon the Lord, than in confessing Him on such occasions. Sometimes I have, by grace, had much real boldness; but often I have manifested the greatest weakness, doing no more than refraining entirely from unholy conversation, without, however, speaking a single word for Him who toiled beyond measure for me. No other remedy do I know for myself and any of my fellow-saints who are weak, like myself, in this particular, than to seek to have the heart so full of Jesus, and to live so in the realization of what He has done for us, that, without any effort, out of the full heart, we may speak for Him.--I found my dear family in peace.

May 8. This evening I went to the prayer meeting at Gideon. I read Psalm ciii, and was able to thank the Lord publicly for my late affliction. This is the first time that I have taken any part in the public meetings of the brethren, since November 6th, 1837.

May 13. Today I was much helped in expounding the Scriptures publicly. When I began I knew not how the Lord would deal with me, whether I should be able to speak or not, as my head is still very weak. But the Lord helped me. I did not feel any loss of mental power. How gracious of the Lord to allow me again to commence serving Him in the ministry of His word.--[For several months after this I preached, on the whole, with much more enjoyment, and with much more earnestness and prayerfulness, than I did before I was taken ill. I also felt more the solemnity of the work.]

June 11. A stranger called on me, and told me, that, many years ago, he had defrauded two gentlemen of a small sum, and that he wished to restore the same with interest. He also stated that he had read my Narrative, and, feeling confidence in me, he requested me to convey this money to those gentlemen, giving me, at the same time, their names and place of abode. He intrusted me with four sovereigns for each of them. At the same time he gave me one sovereign for myself, as a token of Christian love. I never saw the individual before, nor do I up to this moment know his name. I conveyed this money, however, not by post, as he wished but through two bank orders, in order that thus I might be able to show, should it be needful, that I actually did send the money; for in all such matters it becomes one to act with particular caution.--It may be that this fact will be read by some who have, like this stranger, before their conversion, defrauded certain individuals. If so, let them like him, or like Zaccheus of old, restore what they took, and, if they have the means, with interest, or compound interest.

June 13. Last evening my dear wife was taken ill. Often had I prayed respecting her hour, and now was the time to look out for the answer. She continued in most severe sufferings from a little after nine until midnight. Thus hour after hour passed away, until eleven this morning. Another medical attendant was then called in, at the desire of the one who attended her. At three in the afternoon she was delivered of a still-born child.--The whole of the night I was in prayer, as far as my strength allowed me. I cried at last for MERCY, and God heard.

June 14. My dearest wife is alive, but I am depending upon God for her life every moment. She is in much peace. A sister gave me this evening 5l. on account of dear Mary's illness.--[Again we had not thought it well to make pecuniary provision for this time, though at no period of my life had I more abundant means of doing so than during the last few months; but our gracious Father helped us abundantly in this and in other instances, as I shall mention below.]

June 22. Today there was sent to us anonymously, by post, 5l. for our own personal expenses, at this the time of our affliction, when our expenses are so great. The donor accompanied the 5l. note with an affectionate letter to my wife and myself.

July 6. My dear wife, who for more than a fortnight after her delivery was so ill, that the two medical attendants came twice or three times daily, seems now, humanly speaking, likely to recover, and to be given back to me as from the dead. Lord, help me so to receive her!

July 12. From the commencement of the establishment of the Orphan-houses, up to the end of June 1838, the hand of the Lord was seen in the abundance with which He was pleased to supply me with the means for maintaining nearly 100 persons. Now, however, the time is come when "the Father of the fatherless" will show His especial care over them in another way.--The funds, which were this day twelvemonth about 780l., are now reduced to about 20l.; but, thanks be to the Lord, my faith is as strong, or stronger, than it was when we had the larger sum in hand; nor has He at any time, from the commencement of the work, allowed me to distrust Him. Nevertheless, as our Lord will be inquired of, and as real faith is manifested as such by leading to prayer, I gave myself to prayer with brother T---- of the Boy's Orphan-House, who had called on me, and who, besides my wife, and brother Craik, is the only individual to whom I speak about the state of the funds. While we were praying, an orphan child from Frome was brought, and some believers at Frome, having collected among them 5l., sent this money with the child. Thus we received the first answer at a time of need. We have given notice for seven children to come in, and purpose to give notice for five more, though our funds are so low, hoping that God will look on our necessities. [Observe how gently the Lord dealt with us, in that, when want approached, He helped at once, in immediate answer to prayer, in order thus to increase our confidence in Him; but, at the same time, to prepare us for sharper trials of our faith.]

June 17 and 18. These two days we have had two especial prayer meetings, from 6 to 9 in the evening, to commend publicly to the Lord the Boys' Orphan-House. The meetings had been deferred until now, on account of my illness. In the morning of the 18th I expounded, with especial reference to children, 1 Samuel iii., before above 550 children, being our Orphan and Day-School children, and, as many as could come, of those belonging to the Sunday-School. What a great work! What an honour to be allowed to provide Scriptural instruction for so many little ones. Lord, help me to make use of my talents for the benefit of the rising generation, and let me serve my generation according to Thy will!---Our funds for the Orphans are now very low. There are about 20l. in hand, and in a few days 30l. at least will be needed; but I purposely avoided saying any thing about our present necessities, and spoke only, to the praise of God, about the abundance with which our gracious Father, "The Father of the fatherless," has hitherto supplied us. This was done in order that the hand of God, in sending help, may be so much the more clearly seen.

July 22. This evening I was walking in our little garden, meditating on Heb. xiii. 8, "Jesus Christ the same yesterday, and today, and for ever." Whilst meditating on His unchangeable love, power, wisdom, &c.--and turning all, as I went on, into prayer respecting myself; and whilst applying likewise His unchangeable love, and power, and wisdom, &c., both to my present spiritual and temporal circumstances:--- all at once the present need of the Orphan-Houses was brought to my mind. Immediately I was led to say to myself, Jesus in His love and power has hitherto supplied me with what I have needed for the Orphans, and in the same unchangeable love and power He will provide me with what I may need for the future. A flow of joy came into my soul whilst realizing thus the unchangeableness of our adorable Lord. About one minute after, a letter was brought me, enclosing a bill for 20l. In it was written: "Will you apply the amount of the enclosed bill to the furtherance of the objects of your Scriptural Knowledge Society, or of your Orphan Establishment, or in the work and cause of our Master in any way that He Himself, on your application to Him, may point out to you. It is not a great sum, but it is a sufficient provision for the exigency of today; and it is for today's exigencies, that, ordinarily, the Lord provides. Tomorrow, as it brings its demands, will find its supply, etc." [Of this 20l. I took 10l. for the Orphan fund, and 10l. for the other objects, and was thus enabled to meet the expenses of about 34l. which, in connection with the Orphan-Houses, came upon me within four days afterwards, and which I knew beforehand would come.]

On July 26 sailed from Liverpool for the East Indies, for Missionary service, twelve German brethren and three sisters, as the result of the journey of brother ---- and myself to the Continent, in April last.

July 27. Yesterday the funds for the Orphans were reduced to 5l. Blessed be God, my confidence in Him was unshaken! I received yesterday 2l. 13s. Today I was going with my family for change of air to Durdham Down, and thought it well, therefore, to take out any money which there might be in the Orphan-Box in my house. When I opened it, I found a ten pound note and three half crowns. I had been waiting on God for means, both yesterday and today, and thus He has again shown how willing He is to help.

Aug. 6. During this week I shall have to pay again at least 35l. for the Orphans, and have but about 19l. towards it. My eyes are up to the "Father of the fatherless." I believe He will help, though I knew not how.

Aug. 7. How graciously has the Lord again appeared, and that in so short a time! How has he sent help, from altogether unexpected quarters! I have been praying yesterday and today earnestly, beseeching the Lord now to appear, and show His power, that the enemies might not say, "Where is now thy God?" I reminded Him especially, that I had commenced the work that it might be seen, that He, even in our day, is willing to answer prayer, and that the provision for our Orphans might be a visible proof to all around us of this truth. And now observe! Last evening brother Craik told me that 10l. had been given him for the work in our hands; 5l. for the Orphans, and 5l. for the School--Bible--and Missionary fund. Today, having to pay 25l., and not having quite enough, when I went to brother T---- for the money which he might have received, as I knew that 25s. had been given to him, I took with me the keys of the boxes in the Orphan-Houses, to see whether the Lord had sent in a little. I opened the box in the Boys'-Orphan-House, and found 1l. 7s. 5 1/2d. Immediately after I received from brother T---- 13l. 19s. 10d., the greater part of which, as he told me, had come in within the last few days. Thus our adorable Lord has once more delivered; for I have now even more than enough to meet the current expenses of this week.

Aug. 16. When today the account books of the Boys'-Orphan-House were brought, several days sooner than I had expected them, it was found that there was 1l. 6s. 6d. due to the matron. Besides this, money was to be advanced for house-keeping, and there was only 13s. 5 1/2d. in hand. To this one of those connected with the work added 2l. This 2l. 13s. 5 1/2d. was sent to the matron, whilst we were waiting upon God to send more help. In the evening the boxes at the Girls' and Infant-Orphan-Houses were opened, and in them was found 3l. 7s. 5 1/2d. Thus the Lord has kindly helped us again for two or three days.

Aug. 18. I have not one penny in hand for the Orphans. In a day or two again many pounds will be needed. My eyes are up to the Lord. Evening. Before this day is over, I have received from a sister 5l. She had some time since put away her trinkets, to be sold for the benefit of the Orphans. This morning, whilst in prayer, it came to her mind, I have this 5l., and owe no man any thing, therefore it would be better to give this money at once, as it may be some time, before I can dispose of the trinkets. She therefore brought it, little knowing that there was not a penny in hand, and that I had been able to advance only 4l. 15s. 5d. for housekeeping in the Boys'-Orphan-House, instead of the usual 10l.; little knowing also, that within a few days many pounds more will be needed. May my soul be greatly encouraged by this fresh token of my gracious Lord's faithfulness!

Aug. 20. The 5l. which I had received on the 18th, had been given for house-keeping, so that today I was again penniless. But my eyes were up to the Lord. I gave myself to prayer this morning, knowing that I should want again this week at least 13l., if not above 20l. Today I received 12l. in answer to prayer, from a lady who is staying at Clifton, whom I had never seen before. Adorable Lord, grant that this may be a fresh encouragement to me.

Aug. 23. Today I was again without one single penny, when 3l. was sent from Clapham, with a box of new clothes for the Orphans.

Aug. 29. Today sixteen believers were baptized. Of all the baptisms which we have had, this was, perhaps, the most remarkable. Among those who were baptized was an aged brother of above 84 years, and one above 70. For the latter his believing wife had prayed 38 years, and at last the Lord answered her prayers in his conversion. Should any believer who may read this, be on the point of growing weary in prayer for his unconverted relatives, because of the answer being delayed, the above fact may be instrumental in stirring up such a one to give himself to prayer with renewed earnestness and strengthened expectation. "In due season we shall reap, if we faint not." There were also amongst those who were baptized a blind brother and sister, and two very young persons.

Aug. 31. I have been waiting on the Lord for means, as the matron's books from the Girls'-Orphan-House have been brought, and there is no money in hand to advance for house-keeping. But as yet the Lord has not been pleased to send help. As the matron called today for money, one of the labourers gave 2l. of his own, for the present necessities.

Sept. 1. The Lord in His wisdom and love has not yet sent help. Whence it is to come, need not be my care. But I believe God will, in due time, send help. His hour is not yet come. As there was money needed in the Boys'-Orphan-House also, the same brother, just alluded to, gave 2l. for that also. Thus we were delivered at this time likewise. But now his means are gone. This is the most trying hour that as yet I have had in the work, as it regards means; but I know that I shall yet praise the Lord for His help. I have mentioned my arguments before Him, and my gracious Lord, "the Father of the fatherless," will send help.

Sept. 3. This morning the Lord again helped by 2l., which another labourer connected with the work gave. This 2l., together with sixpence which had been given anonymously, was sent off to the Girls'-Orphan-House, where all the money must be gone. There came in further 1l. 14s. 8d. in the course of the day, which was given to the matron of the Boys'-Orphan-House.

Sept. 5. Our hour of trial continues still. The Lord mercifully has given enough to supply our daily necessities; but He gives by the day now, and almost by the hour, as we need it. Nothing came in yesterday. I have besought the Lord again and again, both yesterday and today. It is as if the Lord said: "Mine hour is not yet come." But I have faith in God. I believe that He surely will send help, though I know not whence it is to come. Many pounds are needed within a few days, and there is not a penny in hand. This morning 2l. was given for the present necessities, by one of the labourers in the work.--Evening: This very day the Lord sent again some help to encourage me to continue to wait on Him, and to trust in Him. As I was praying this afternoon respecting the matter, I felt fully assured that the Lord would send help, and praised Him beforehand for His help, and asked Him to encourage our hearts through it. I have been also led yesterday and today to ask the Lord especially, that He would not allow my faith to fail. A few minutes after I had prayed, brother T---- came and brought 4l. 1s. 5d., which had come in, in several small donations. He told me, at the same time, that tomorrow the books will be brought from the Infant-Orphan-House, when money must be advanced for housekeeping. I thought for a moment, it might be well to keep 3l. of this money for that purpose. But it occurred to me immediately, "Sufficient unto the day is the evil thereof." The Lord can provide, by tomorrow, much more than I need, and I therefore sent 3l. to one of the sisters, whose quarterly salary was due, and the remaining 1l. 1s. 5d. to the Boys'-Orphan-House for housekeeping. Thus I am still penniless. My hope is in God: He will provide.

Sept. 6. This morning the books were brought from the Infant-Orphan-House, and the matron sent to ask when she should fetch them, implying, when they would have been looked over, and when money would be advanced for housekeeping. I said "tomorrow," though I had not a single penny in hand. About an hour after, brother T---- sent me a note, to say that he had received 1l. this morning, and that last evening a brother had sent 29lbs. of salt, 44 dozen of onions, and 26lbs. of groats.

Sept. 7. The time had come that I had to send money to the Infant-Orphan-House, but the Lord had not sent any more. I gave, therefore, the 1l. which had come in yesterday, and 2s. 2d. which had been put into the box in my house, trusting to the good Lord to send in more.

Sept. 8. Saturday evening. I am still in the hour of probation. It has not pleased my gracious Lord to send me help as yet.--The evening before last I heard brother Craik preach on Genesis xii., about Abraham's faith. He showed how all went on well, as long as Abraham acted in faith, and walked according to the will of God; and how all failed when he distrusted God. Two points I felt particularly important in my case. 1. That I may not go any by-ways, or ways of my own, for deliverance. I have about 220l. in the bank, which, for other purposes in the Lord's work, has been entrusted to me by a brother and a sister. I might take of this money, and say but to the sister--and write but to the brother, that I have taken, in these my straits, 20l., 50l., or 100l., for the Orphans, and they would be quite satisfied (for both of them have liberally given for the Orphans, and the brother has more than once told me, only to let him know when I wanted money;) but this would be a deliverance of my own, not God's deliverance. Besides, it would be no small barrier to the exercise of faith, in the next hour of trial. 2. I was particularly reminded afresh, in hearing brother Craik, of the danger of dishonouring the Lord in that very way in which I have, through His grace, in some small measure brought glory to Him, even by trusting in Him.--Yesterday and today I have been pleading with God eleven arguments, why He would be graciously pleased to send help. My mind has been in peace respecting the matter. Yesterday the peace amounted even to joy in the Holy Ghost But this I must say, that the burden of my prayer, during the last days, has been chiefly, that the Lord in mercy would keep my faith from failing. My eyes are up to Him. He can help soon. One thing I am sure of: In His own way, and in His own time He will help. The arguments which I plead with God are:

1. That I set about the work for the glory of God, i e. that there might be a visible proof, by God supplying, in answer to prayer only, the necessities of the Orphans, that He is the living God, and most willing, even in our day, to answer prayer; and that, therefore, He would be pleased to send supplies.

2. That God is the "Father of the fatherless," and that He, therefore, as their Father, would be pleased to provide. Psalm lxviii. 5.

3. That I have received the children in the name of Jesus, and that, therefore, He, in these children, has been received, and is fed, and is clothed; and that, therefore, He would be pleased to consider this. Mark ix. 36, 37.

4. That the faith of many of the children of God has been strengthened by this work hitherto, and that, if God were to withhold the means for the future, those who are weak in faith would be staggered; whilst by a continuance of means, their faith might still further be strengthened.

5. That many enemies would laugh, were the Lord to withhold supplies, and say, did we not foretell that this enthusiasm would come to nothing?

6. That many of the children of God, who are uninstructed, or in a carnal state, would feel themselves justified to continue their alliance with the world in the work of God, and to go on as heretofore, in their unscriptural proceedings respecting similar institutions, so far as the obtaining of means is concerned, if He were not to help me.

7. That the Lord would remember that I am His child, and that He would graciously pity me, and remember that I cannot provide for these children, and that therefore He would not allow this burden to lie upon me long without sending help.

8. That He would remember likewise my fellow-labourers in the work, who trust in Him, but who would be tried were He to withhold supplies.

9. That He would remember that I should have to dismiss the children from under our Scriptural instruction to their former companions.

10. That He would show, that those were mistaken who said, that, at the first, supplies might be expected, while the thing was new, but not afterwards.

11. That I should not know, were He to withhold means, what construction I should put upon all the many most remarkable answers to prayer, which He had given me heretofore in connexion with this work, and which most fully have shown to me that it is of God.

In some small measure I now understand, experimentally, the meaning of that word "how long," which so frequently occurs in the prayers of the Psalms. But even now, by the grace of God, my eyes are up unto Him only, and I believe that He will send help.

Sept. 10. Monday morning. Neither Saturday nor yesterday had any money come in. It appeared to me now needful to take some steps on account of our need, i.e., to go to the Orphan Houses, call the brethren and sisters together, (who, except brother T----, had never been informed about the state of the funds), state the case to them, see how much money was needed for the present, tell them that amidst all this trial of faith I still believed that God would help, and to pray with them. Especially, also, I meant to go for the sake of telling them that no more articles must be purchased than we have the means to pay for, but to let there be nothing lacking in any way to the children, as it regards nourishing food and needful clothing; for I would rather at once send them away than that they should lack. I meant to go for the sake also of seeing whether there were still articles remaining which had been sent for the purpose of being sold, or whether there were any articles really needless, that we might turn them into money. I felt that the matter was now come to a solemn crisis.-- About half-past nine six-pence came in, which had been put anonymously into the box at Gideon Chapel. This money seemed to me like an earnest, that God would have compassion and send more. About ten, after I had returned from brother Craik, to whom I had unbosomed my heart again, whilst once more in prayer for help, a sister called who gave two sovereigns to my wife for the Orphans, stating that she had felt herself stirred up to come, and that she had delayed coming already too long. A few minutes after, when I went into the room where she was, she gave me two sovereigns more, and all this without knowing the least about our need. Thus the Lord most mercifully has sent us a little help, to the great encouragement of my faith. A few minutes after I was called on for money from the Infant-Orphan-House, to which I sent 2l., and 1l. 0s. 6d. to the Boys'-Orphan-House, and 1l. to the Girls'-Orphan-House.

Brother Craik left Bristol today for a few days in company with another brother. I should have gone with them for the sake of obtaining some quiet for my head; but I must remain, to pass with my dear Orphans through the trial; though these dear little ones know nothing about it, because their tables are as well supplied as when there was 800l. in the bank, and they have lack of nothing.

Today I saw a young brother who, as well as one of his sisters, had been brought to the knowledge of the Lord through my Narrative.

Sept. 11. The good Lord, in His wisdom, still sees it needful to keep us very low. But this afternoon brother T---- called, and told me that one of our fellow-labourers had sold his metal watch, and two gold pins, for 1l. 1s., that 9s. 6d. had come in, and that two of our fellow-labourers had sent two lots of books of their own, 19 and 21 in number, to be sold for the Orphans. What an abundant blessing, that in such a season of trial I have such fellow-labourers! This 1l. 10s. 6d. was given to the Boys'-Orphan-House.

Sept. 12. Still the trial continues. Only 9s. came in today, given by one of the labourers. In the midst of this great trial of faith the Lord still mercifully keeps me in great peace. He also allows me to see, that our labour is not in vain; for yesterday died Leah Culliford, one of the orphans, about 9 years old, truly converted, and brought to the faith some months before her departure.

Sept. 13. No help has come yet. This morning found it was absolutely needful to tell the brethren and sisters about the state of the funds, and to give necessary directions as to not going into debt, etc. We prayed together, and had a very happy meeting. They all seemed comfortable 12s. 6d. was taken out of the boxes in the three houses, 12s. one of the labourers gave, and 1l. 1s. had come in for needlework done by the children.

One of the sisters, who is engaged in the work, sent a message after me, not to trouble myself about her salary, for she should not want any for a twelvemonth. What a blessing to have such fellow-labourers!

Sept. 14. I met again this morning with the brethren and sisters for prayer, as the Lord has not yet sent help. After prayer one of the labourers gave me all the money he had, 16s., saying that it would not be upright to pray, if he were not to give what he had. One of the sisters told me, that in six days she would give 6l., which she had in the Savings' Bank for such a time of need. God be praised for such fellow-labourers!---Up to this day the matrons of the three houses had been in the habit of paying the bakers and the milkman weekly, because they had preferred to receive the payments in this way, and sometimes it had thus been also with the butcher and grocer. But now, as the Lord deals out to us by the day, we considered it would be wrong to go on any longer in this way, as the week's payment might become due, and we have no money to meet it; and thus those with whom we deal might be inconvenienced by us, and we be found acting against the commandment of the Lord, "Owe no man anything." Rom. xiii. 8. From this day, and hence-forward, whilst the Lord gives to us our supplies by the day, we purpose therefore to pay at once for every article as it is purchased, and never to buy anything except we can pay for it at once, however much it may seem to be needed, and however much those with whom we deal may wish to be paid only by the week. The little which was owed was paid off this day.--When I came home I found a large parcel of new clothes, which had been sent from Dublin for the Orphans, a proof that tire Lord remembers us still. We met again in the evening for prayer. We were of good cheer, and still BELIEVE that the Lord will supply our need.

Sept. 15. Saturday. We met again this morning for prayer. God comforts our hearts. We are looking for help. I found that there were provisions enough for today and tomorrow, but there was no money in hand to take in bread as usual, in order that the children might not have newly baked bread. This afternoon one of the labourers, who had been absent for several days from Bristol, returned, and gave 1l. This evening we met again for prayer, when I found that 10s. 6d. more had come in since the morning. With this 1l. 10s. 6d. we were able to buy, even this Saturday evening, the usual quantity of bread, (as it might be difficult to get stale bread on Monday morning,) and have some money left. God be praised, who gave us grace to come to the decision not to take any bread today, as usual, nor to buy any thing for which we cannot pay at once. We were very comfortable, thankfully taking this money out of our Father's hands, as a proof that He still cares for us, and that, in His own time, He will send us larger sums.

Today, a brother kindly paid the bill for medical attendance on my dear wife during her confinement. The same brother also had paid, some weeks since, the second medical attendant, who was called in. Thus the Lord, in various ways, sends help to us, showing continually His fatherly care over us.

Sept. 16. Lord's day afternoon. We met again for prayer respecting supplies for the Orphans. We are in peace, and our hope is in God, that He graciously will appear, though but one shilling has come in since last evening.

Sept. 17. The trial still continues. It is now more and more trying, even to faith, as each day comes. Truly, the Lord has wise purposes in allowing us to call so long upon Him for help. But I am sure God will send help, if we can but wait. One of the labourers had had a little money come in, of which he gave 12s. 6d.; another labourer gave 11s. 8d., being all the money she had left: this, with 17s. 6d., which, partly, had come in, and, partly, was in hand, enabled us to pay what needed to be paid, and to purchase provisions, so that nothing yet, in any way, has been lacking. This evening I was rather tried respecting the long delay of larger sums coming; but being led to go to the Scriptures for comfort, my soul was greatly refreshed, and my faith again strengthened, by the xxxivth Psalm, so that I went very cheerfully to meet with my dear fellow-labourers for prayer. I read to them the Psalm, and sought to cheer their hearts through the precious promises contained in it.

Sept. 18. Brother T. had 25s. in hand, and I had 3s. This 1l. 8s. enabled us to buy the meat and bread, which was needed; a little tea for one of the houses, and milk for all; no more than this is needed. Thus the Lord has provided not only for this day, but there is bread for two days in hand. Now, however, we are come to an extremity. The funds are exhausted. The labourers, who had a little money, have given as long as they had any left.--Now observe how the Lord helped us! A lady from the neighbourhood of London who brought a parcel with money from her daughter, arrived four or five days since in Bristol, and took lodgings next door to the Boys' Orphan-House. This afternoon she herself kindly brought me the money, amounting to 3l. 2s. 6d. We had been reduced so low as to be on the point of selling those things which could be spared; but this morning I had asked the Lord, if it might be, to prevent the necessity of our doing so. That the money had been so near the Orphan-Houses for several days without being given, is a plain proof that it was from the beginning in the heart of God to help us; but, because He delights in the prayers of His children, He had allowed us to pray so long; also to try our faith, and to make the answer so much the sweeter. It is indeed a precious deliverance. I burst out into loud praises and thanks the first moment I was alone, after I had received the money. I met with my fellow-labourers again this evening for prayer and praise; their hearts were not a little cheered. This money was this evening divided, and will comfortably provide for all that will be needed tomorrow.

Sept. 20. Morning. The Lord has again kindly sent in a little. Last evening was given to me 1s. 6d., and this morning 1l. 3s. Evening. This evening the Lord sent still further supplies; 8l. 11s. 2 1/2d. came in, as a further proof that the Lord is not unmindful of us. There was in the box of the Girls' Orphan-House 1l. 1s., and in that of the Boys' Orphan-House 1l. 7s. 2 1/2d. One of the labourers, in accordance with her promise this day week, gave 6l. 3s. About eighteen months ago she saw it right no longer to have money for herself in the Savings' Bank, and she therefore, in her heart, gave the money which she had there to the Orphan-Houses, intending to draw it in a time of need. Some time since (she told me this evening) she drew a part of it to buy several useful articles for the Orphan-Houses; now the sum was reduced to 6l. When she found out the present need, she went this day week to the Savings'

Bank, and gave notice that she wished to draw her money today. Truly, as long as God shall be pleased to give me such fellow-labourers, His blessing will rest upon the work! This 8l. 11s. 2 1/2d. was divided this evening to supply the three houses, and we thanked God, unitedly, for His help.

Sept. 22. Both yesterday and today we have again assembled for prayer and praise. We are in no immediate want, but on the 29th 19l. 10s. will be due for the rent of the three Orphan-Houses.--Today there was only 4s. 7d. in hand for the other objects of the Institution, though it was the pay-day for some of the teachers. My comfort was the living God. During this week He had helped me so repeatedly and in such a remarkable way, as it regards the Orphan-Houses, that it would have been doubly sinful not to have trusted in Him for help under this fresh difficulty. No money came in this morning. About two, the usual time when the teachers are paid, a sovereign was given, with which I went immediately to brother T. (who attends to this part of the work), to pay at least in part, the weekly salaries. I found that he had received a sovereign in the morning. By means of this sovereign, together with the one which I had received just at the moment when it was needed, we were helped through this day.

Sept. 25. Yesterday and the previous days we have continued to assemble for prayer. In four days the rent for the Orphan-Houses will be due, and we have nothing towards it; also, the housekeeping money in the three houses is now again gone. May the Lord have compassion on us, and continue to send us help! A little came in this morning: there was found 9s. 6d. in the box in my house.

Sept. 27. The 9s. 6d. which came in the day before yesterday, was given to the Infant-Orphan-House. Thus we were helped through that day and yesterday. There was every thing that was needed in the three houses; I had made particular enquiry; there was meat even for today. We met yesterday again for prayer. Today I was not able to go, on account of indisposition; I sent, therefore, to brother T. to request him to divide the 18s. 6d., (10s. of which had come in last evening, and 8s. 6d. of which we had in hand), between the three matrons. This afternoon I hear of a fresh deliverance which the Lord has wrought. About five weeks ago, a farmer applied for the admission of an orphan-girl, his grand-daughter. As I knew, however, that he had the means of providing for her, and as our Institution is only for destitute orphans, I informed him that the child could only be received, on condition of his paying 10l. a year for her support, (which is about the average expense for the younger girls), and this, quarterly, in advance.4 This morning he came, brought the child, and paid 2l. 10s. in advance, and gave 1l. besides. Thus the Lord has again most seasonably helped us in this our time of need. May He keep the memory of these deliverances alive in our souls, and increase our confidence in Him by every fresh one! In less than two days we have to pay 19l. 10s. for rent! May the Lord keep us looking to Him, and mercifully send help!

Sept. 29. Saturday evening. Prayer has been made for several days past respecting the rent, which is due this day. I have been looking out for it, though I knew not whence a shilling was to come. This morning brother T. called on me, and, as no money had come in, we prayed together, and continued in supplication from ten till a quarter to twelve. Twelve o'clock struck (the time when the rent ought to have been paid), but no money had been sent. For some days past I have repeatedly had a misgiving, whether the Lord might not disappoint us, in order that we might be led to provide by the week, or the day, for the rent. This is the second, and only the second, complete failure as to answers of prayer in the work, during the past four years and six months. The first was about the half-yearly rent of Castle-Green school-room, due July 1, 1837, which had come in only in part by that time. I am now fully convinced that the rent ought to be put by daily or weekly, as God may prosper us, in order that the work, even as to this point, may be a testimony. May the Lord, then, help us to act accordingly; and may He now mercifully send in the means to pay the rent!--Whilst in this matter our prayers have failed, either to humble us, or to show us how weak our faith is still, or to teach us, (which seems to me the most probable,) that we ought to provide the rent beforehand; the Lord has given us again fresh proofs, even this day, that He is mindful of us. There was not money enough in the Girls'-Orphan-House to take in bread, (we give the bread to the children on the third day after it is baked); but before the baker came, a lady called who had had some needlework done by the children, and paid 3s. 11d., and thus the matron was able to take in bread as usual. I found this morning 2s. in the box in my house, our extremity having led me to look into it. One of the labourers gave 13s. This 15s. was divided amongst the three matrons. Thanks to the Lord, there is all which is needed for today and tomorrow.

Sept. 30. We are not only poor as regards the Orphan-fund, but also the funds for the other objects bring us again and again to the Lord for fresh supplies. Today, when we had not a single penny in hand, 5l. was given for the other objects.

Oct. 2. Tuesday evening. The Lord's holy name be praised! He hath dealt most bountifully with us during the last three days! The day before yesterday 5l. came in for the Orphans. Of this I gave to each house 10s. which supplied them before the provisions were consumed. Oh! how kind is the Lord. Always, before there has been actual want, He has sent help. Yesterday came in 1l. 10s. more. This 1l. 10s., with 4s. 2d. in hand, was divided for present necessities. Thus the expenses of yesterday, for housekeeping, were defrayed. The Lord helped me also to pay yesterday the 19l. 10s. for the rent. The means for it were thus obtained. One of the labourers had received through his family 10l., and 5l. besides from a sister in the Lord; also some other money. Of this he gave 16l., which, with the 3l. 10s. that was left of the above-mentioned 5l., which came in the day before yesterday, made up 19l. 10s., the sum which was needed.

--This day we were again greatly reduced. There was no money in hand to take in bread as usual, for the Boys' and Infant Orphan-Houses, but again the Lord helped.

A sister who had arrived this afternoon from Swansea brought 1l. 7s., and one of the labourers sold an article, by means of which he was able to give 1l. 13s. Thus we had 3l.:---1l. for each house, and could buy bread before the day was over. Hitherto we have lacked nothing!

Oct. 4. Thursday. The money of Tuesday helped us through yesterday. Today, when again all was gone, and help was greatly needed, our loving Lord appeared. The books which had been given some time since, by some of my fellow-labourers, were sold for 11s., also an old bedstead for 2s. 6d., and an old sofa for 10s. The boxes were also opened, as I had been told some money had been put in, and 9s. 1d. was found in them. This money was a fresh encouragement to us in our need. By this 1l. 12s. 7d. we were helped through the day.

Oct. 5. This morning, just before I was going to the Orphan-Houses to meet with the brethren and sisters for prayer, 1l. 3s. was brought from Teignmouth. This money seems to have been given some months since to a brother at Teignmouth, but it did not reach me until today. It is a most seasonable help, to defray the expenses of this day, and a fresh proof, that not in anger, but only for the trial of our faith, our gracious Lord delays as yet, to send larger sums.

Oct. 6. Saturday. The Lord has again most kindly helped us. It came to my mind that there were some new blankets in the Orphan-Houses, which had been given some time since, but which are not needed, and might therefore be sold. I was confirmed in this by finding that the moth had got into one pair. I therefore sold ten pairs, having a good opportunity to do so. Thus the Lord not only supplied again our present need for the three houses, but I was also able to put by the rent for this week and the next, acting out the light which He had given us this day week. There came in 9s. 6d., besides 7l. for the blankets. The School fund, also, was again completely exhausted, when today and yesterday came in so much, that not only the weekly salaries could be paid today, but also above 1l. could be put by for rent.

Oct. 9. Through the last-mentioned supplies for the Orphans we were helped up to this day; but today we were brought lower than ever. The provisions would have lasted out only today, and the money for milk in one of the houses could only be made up by one of the labourers selling one of his books. The matron in the Boys'-Orphan-House had this morning two shillings left. When in doubt whether to buy bread with it, or more meat, to make up the dinner with the meat which she had in the house, the baker called, and left three quarterns of bread as a present. In this great need, some money having been given to one of the labourers, he gave 2l. of it, by which we were able to buy meat, bread, and other provisions. Nevertheless even this day, low as we had been brought, before this 2l. was given, there had been all in the house that was needed.

Oct. 10. The Lord had sent in so much since yesterday afternoon, that we were able at our meeting this morning to divide 2l. 0s. 2d. between the three matrons, whereby we are helped through this day. But now the coals in the Infant-Orphan-House are out, and nearly so in the other two houses. Also the treacle casks in all the three houses are nearly empty. On this account we have asked the Lord for fresh supplies.

Oct. 11. The "Father of the fatherless" has again shown his care over us. An Orphan from Devonshire arrived last evening. With her was sent 2l. 5s. 6d. The sister who brought her gave also a silver tea-pot, sugar-basin, and cream jug (of the weight of 48 oz.), having found true riches in Christ. There was also in the boxes 9s. One of the labourers paid for a ton of coals. We obtained 16l. 16s. for the silver articles.-- Thus we were helped through the heavy expenses of the following days.

Oct. 12. Today seven brethren and sisters were added to us in fellowship, and eight were proposed. May the Lord send helpers for the work!

Oct. 13. For three months past the Orphan fund has been low, yet hitherto we have lacked nothing!

Oct. 15. I knew that there would be money needed this morning, for many things in the Orphan-Houses, and my heart was therefore lifted up to the Lord. Just when I was going to meet my fellow labourers for prayer, I received from Trowbridge 4l. There had come in also at the Orphan-Houses 7s. 3d. To this one of the labourers added 1l. Thus I was enabled abundantly to supply all that was wanted, and to pay for a cask of treacle and a ton of coals. We are now, however, cast again on the love of our Lord for further supplies, as there is neither any thing in hand, nor have the labourers any more of their own to give.

Oct. 16. The day commenced with mercies. I was looking up to the Lord for help, early this morning, when, almost immediately afterwards, brother T. came, and brought two silver table-spoons, and six tea-spoons, which had been left, anonymously, yesterday afternoon, at the Girls'-Orphan-House. This afternoon I received 12l. from Staffordshire. On the seal of the letter, which enclosed the money, was "Ebenezer." How true in our case! Surely this instance is a fresh "Ebenezer" to us; for hitherto the Lord has helped us.--There was also found a half sovereign in the box at my house. Also a lady left 5s. at the door of the Girls'-Orphan-House, with about 200 pears for the children; and a brother sent 2s., the first fruits of the increase of his wages. Thus I was able to give a larger supply than usual to the matrons.

Oct. 22. Today our funds were again quite low. In the Infant-Orphan-House only 2d. was left, and very little in the other two houses. But the Lord most manifestly again answered prayer. A gentleman from London, who is greatly interested about destitute and neglected children, came over from Bath with two of his sisters to see

41

the Orphan-Houses. He gave 1l. There was 2s. 6d. put into the box at my house, and 6d. anonymously into the box at Gideon Chapel. With this 1l. 3s. I went directly to the Orphan-Houses to relieve the present need. Whilst I was there, the Lord gave still further supplies; for being informed that in the morning some ladies had seen the houses, and put money into the boxes, I opened them and found 3l. 0s. 1d. Thus the Lord, by means of this 4l. 3s. 1d., helped us through the necessities of this day.

Oct. 23. The Lord again sent above 2l., which supplied this day's necessities.

Oct. 24. Today the Lord sent from a most unexpected quarter 5l. The money was given by a relative of two children in the Boys'-Orphan-House. Thus we are helped for two days, and are able to put by the rent for this week.

Oct. 27. Saturday. This day we have been again mercifully helped, though our need has been almost greater than ever. But, thanks to our adorable Lord! this day also we have not been confounded; for there was 6s. in the box at the Infant-Orphan-House, and 6s. came in for things which had been given to be sold. To this one of the labourers added 18s. By means of this 1l. 10s. we have been able to meet all pressing demands, and to procure provisions for today and tomorrow.

Oct. 29. Monday. The Lord has again given us this day our daily bread, though, in the morning, there was not the least natural prospect of obtaining supplies. One of the labourers, who had received some money for his own personal expenses, gave 2l. Some things also, which had been given for sale, had been sold for 18s.; and 6d. had been put into the box at Gideon Chapel This 2l. 18s. 6d. enabled us to meet the expenses of this day. There were also many articles of worn clothes sent.

Oct. 30. This has been again a day of peculiar mercies in reference to the funds. Whilst I was in prayer respecting them, a brother brought 2 1/4 yards of cloth. He had bought it for himself, but, afterwards considering that he had sufficient clothes, he gave it to be sold for the Orphans. This evening a sister gave me 20l., ten of which were for the Orphans, and ten for the other objects. Thus we are helped for this week.

Nov. 4. Lord's day. There was given, by a stranger, last Wednesday evening, at Bethesda Chapel, to one of the sisters, a sovereign for the Orphans, which I received today. Thus the Lord has again begun the week with mercy, and His love surely will help us through it, though again many pounds will be needed.

Nov. 5. Monday. By means of the sovereign which had come in yesterday, and several small donations today and on the past days, together with 2l. 10s. which one of the labourers added of his own, 6l. 2s. 6d. was divided this day between the three matrons, which will supply their need for two days at least.

Nov. 7. The funds are now again completely exhausted. Today I divided 1l. 3s. 8d., which had come in yesterday; thus the necessary wants were supplied. The Lord be praised who has helped us hitherto! One of the Orphans was sent today to service, and the Lord enabled us to give her a suitable outfit.

Nov. 8. Last evening 1l. 4s. came in, which, being divided between the three houses, helped us through this day.

Nov. 10. Saturday. All seemed to be dark, so far as regards natural appearances, at the commencement of this day. But through this day also the Lord has helped us, and enabled us to meet all demands. In the course of the day came in 1l. 8s. 6d. To this two of the labourers added 10s. each, and thus we were brought to the close of one more week, having been able to supply the necessities of 97 persons in the Orphan-Houses, without owing any thing.

Nov. 12. Monday. Sixpence came in this morning, to which one of the labourers added 10s. 6d., to meet the most pressing necessities. This evening I found the 1l. was not enough to take in bread for the Boys'-Orphan-House. The Lord gave us, however, before the day was over, enough to buy the usual quantity of bread; for there was found in the boxes 5s. 9d. and a pair of small gold earrings.

Nov. 13. This morning our want was again great. I have 20l. in hand which has been put by for rent, but, for the Lord's honour, I would not take of it. Nothing had come in, and the labourers had scarcely any thing to give. I went, however, to the Orphan-Houses, to pray with my fellow labourers, and, if it might be, to comfort them, and see what could be done. When I came there, I found that 19s. 6d. had come in this morning. On enquiry I heard that only 2s. 6d. more was needed to carry us through the day. This one of the labourers was able to add of his own. Thus the Lord has again helped us out of our difficulty. One of the labourers gave some things which he could do without, and another gave a workbox to be sold for the Orphans.-- Before this day has come to an end, the Lord has sent in 1l. 2s. 4d. more, so that we have also a little for tomorrow.

Nov. 15. The money which had come in the day before yesterday, supplied the necessities of yesterday also; but today we were brought again very low. I went to the Orphan-Houses, to pray with my fellow-labourers, not without hope that the Lord might have appeared, and sent a little help. When I arrived I found that one of the labourers had sold a few of his books, together with two which had been given by another labourer on the 13th, for which he had received 7s. To this one of the labourers added 7s. 9d. This 14s. 9d. supplied the most pressing necessities. When I came home I found 1s. in the box at my house, and soon after received 5s. for a pair of fire screens, which had been given for sale. There were also three baskets of potatoes sent to the three different houses. A sack of potatoes had been ordered, but the brother, who had been desired to bring them, could not conveniently do so today, and thought, as this present had been ordered from him, there would be no immediate need of them; and Oh! how kind of the Lord to order it thus: for had he brought them, the payment would have taken away the money which was intended for the usual quantity of bread. But before the day was over, the Lord helped still further. In the afternoon a gentleman from Bath called at the Boys'-Orphan-House, and gave a cheque for 3l. There was also 1s. given; 2s. 6d. came in for needle-work, and 5s. 6d. for things sold. Thus altogether 4l. 4s. 9d. has been sent by the Lord this day.

Nov. 17. Saturday. Today above 3l. was needed, and as only 15s. 6d. had come in, we found it needful to determine to dispose of a few articles of furniture which we conveniently could do without. One of the labourers gave a good watch to be sold, which she had bought some months since, there being then no time-piece in one of the houses. In consideration of these articles to be sold, I took, for the present necessities of the Orphans, 2l. 10s. of the money which had been put by for the rent, to be replaced when these articles could be sold at a suitable opportunity. Thus we were helped to the close of one more week.

Nov. 19. Today we were again in great need. There had come in only 7s. 6d. for needle-work. The Lord had, however, given to one of the labourers a little money, of which he gave 15s., by means of which we were helped through this day also.

Nov. 20. Today our need was exceedingly great, but the Lord's help was great also. I went to meet with the brethren and sisters as usual. I found that 1l. would be needed to supply the necessities of today, but 3s. only had come in. Just when we were going to pray, one of the labourers came in, who, after prayer, gave 10s. Whilst we were praying, another labourer came in, who had received 1l. Thus we had 1l. 13s.; even more, therefore, than was absolutely needed.

Nov. 21. Never were we so reduced in funds as today. There was not a single halfpenny in hand between the matrons of the three houses. Nevertheless there was a good dinner, and, by managing so as to help one another with bread, etc., there was a prospect of getting over this day also; but for none of the houses had we the prospect of being able to take in bread. When I left the brethren and sisters at one o'clock, after prayer, I told them that we must wait for help, and see how the Lord would deliver us at this time. I was sure of help, but we were indeed straitened. When I came to Kingsdown, I felt that I needed more exercise, being very cold; wherefore I went not the nearest way home, but round by Clarenceplace. About twenty yards from my house, I met a brother who walked back with me, and after a little conversation gave me 10l. to be handed over to the brethren, the deacons, towards providing the poor saints with coals, blankets and warm clothing; also 5l. for the Orphans, and 5l. for the other objects of the Scriptural Knowledge Institution. The brother had called twice while I was gone to the Orphan-Houses, and had I now been one half minute later, I should have missed him. But the Lord knew our need, and therefore allowed me to meet him. I sent off the 5l. immediately to the matrons.

Nov. 23. The above-mentioned 5l., with an addition of 11s. 6d. which had also come in, helped us through the expenses of yesterday and today.

Nov. 24. This again has been a very remarkable day. We had as little in hand this morning as at any time, and yet several pounds were needed. But God, who is rich in mercy, and whose word so positively declares that none who trust in Him shall be confounded, has helped us through this day also. While I was in prayer, about ten in the morning, respecting the funds, I was informed that a gentleman had called to see me. He came to inform me that a lady had ordered three sacks of potatoes to be sent to the Orphan Houses. Never could they have come more seasonably. This was an encouragement to me, to continue to expect help. When I came to the prayer meeting about 12 o'clock, I heard that 2s. had come in, also 1l. for a guitar, which had been given for sale. The payment for this guitar had been expected for many weeks. It had been mentioned among us, repeatedly, that it might come just at a time, when we most needed it: and oh! how true. Also the watch which had been given was sold for 2l. 10s. But with all this we could not have put by the rents for this week, amounting to 30s. One of the labourers, therefore, gave his watch to the Orphan-fund under this condition, that should the Lord not enable us before Dec. 21st to make up this deficiency, it should be sold, but not otherwise, as he needs it in the Lord's service.-- [A few days after the Lord gave the means to put by the 30s., and 30s. besides for the next week's rent.] Thus the Lord helped us through this day, and with it brought us to the close of one more week.

Nov. 25. Lord's-day. The Lord kindly remembers us before there is absolute need. A sister who is going to leave Bristol, called on me to bid me farewell, and gave me, in parting, 1l. 10s. for the Orphans. It is remarkable, that almost every donation given within the last four months and thirteen days, since our funds have been low, has come from unexpected quarters, to make the hand of God so much the more manifest.

Nov. 26. Though there had come in yesterday 1l. 10s., yet that was scarcely the half of what was needed this day. But the Lord knew our circumstances, and, as He is wont to do, most unworthy as we are of it, remembered our need. There was given 1l. this morning, and 1s. had been put anonymously into the box at Gideon Chapel; and a lamp, which had been given some time since, had been sold for 10s. Also 1s. 2d. came in for needlework. By means of these several little sums we could meet all the demands of this day.

Nov. 27. Yesterday afternoon came in 10s., and this morning, by the disposal of some articles, which had been given for sale, 12s. This furnished us with means to procure, for this day also, the necessary supplies.

Nov. 28. This is, perhaps, of all days the most remarkable as yet, so far as it regards the funds. When I was in prayer this morning respecting them, I was enabled firmly to believe that the Lord would send help, though all seemed dark as to natural appearances. At 12 o'clock I met as usual with the brethren and sisters for prayer. There had come in only 1s., which was left last evening anonymously, at the Infant Orphan-House, and which, except 2d., had already been spent, on account of the great need. I heard also that an individual had gratuitously cleaned the time-piece in the Infant Orphan-House, and had offered to keep the timepieces of the three houses in repair. Thus the Lord gave even in this a little encouragement, and a proof that He is still mindful of us. On inquiry I found that there was every thing needful for the dinner in all the three houses; but neither in the Infant nor Boys' Orphan-Houses was there bread enough for tea, nor money to buy milk. Lower we had never been, and, perhaps, never so low. We gave ourselves now unitedly to prayer, laying the case in simplicity before the Lord. Whilst in prayer there was a knock at the door, and one of the sisters went out. After the two brethren, who labour in the Orphan-Houses, and I had prayed aloud, we continued for a while silently in prayer. As to myself, I was lifting up my heart to the Lord to make a way for our escape, and in order to know, if there were any other thing which I could do with a good conscience, besides waiting on Him, so that we might have food for the children. At last we rose from our knees. I said, "God will surely send help." The words had not quite passed over my lips, when I perceived a letter lying on the table, which had been brought whilst we were in prayer. It was from my wife, containing another letter from a brother with 10l. for the Orphans. The evening before last I was asked by a brother whether the balance in hand for the Orphans would be as great this time, when the accounts would be made up, as the last time. My answer was, that it would be as great as the Lord pleased. The next morning this brother was moved to remember the Orphans, and to send today 10l., which arrived after I had left my house, and which on account of our need was forwarded immediately to me. Thus I was enabled to give 6l. 10s. for housekeeping, and to put by 3l. 10s. for rent.

The brother who sent the 10l. for the Orphans, sent likewise 10l. to be divided between brother Craik and me, with the object of purchasing new clothes for ourselves.

Nov. 29. The Lord has greatly blessed our meetings for prayer. They have been instrumental in leading us to much prayer for the children in the Orphan-Houses, in the Day-Schools, and in the Sunday-School. They have led us to prayer for ourselves, for the Day-School Teachers, and for the Sunday-School Teachers, that grace may be given to us so to walk before the children, and so to deal with them, as that the Lord may be glorified by us. We have also often been led to intercede for the believers with whom we are in fellowship, and for the Church at large. We have especially prayed, that our work may lead the church generally to a more simple confidence and trust in the Lord. That these meetings have not been in vain, as regards the procuring of funds, has been already sufficiently seen by the many instances which have been recorded in the foregoing pages. Today, however, we have had another particular proof of this. When we met I found that 10s. had come in yesterday afternoon. When I returned home I found 1l. had come in, and shortly after I received another 1l. In the evening I received 50l., which was sent from Suffolk by a sister who had often expressed how gladly she would contribute more largely to the work which is in our hands, had she the means, and who just now, in this our time of need, has obtained the means to carry out the desire of her heart. I rejoice in the last donation particularly, not because of the largeness of the sum, but because it enables me to pay to my brethren and sisters in the Orphan-Houses the salary which is due to them. For though they are willing to labour without any remuneration, nevertheless "the labourer is worthy of his reward." This donation also proves, that the Lord is willing even now, as formerly, to send large sums. But I expect still larger. The same sister who sent the 50l. for the Orphans, sent, at the same time, 30l. to be divided between brother Craik and me for our personal expenses. How abundantly does the Lord care for us! Truly we serve a kind Master!

Dec. 5. Today there were again a few shillings needed, in the Boys' Orphan-House. That which remained of the L50l. had been divided for housekeeping in the three houses, and was now all spent in the Boys' Orphan-House, and nearly also in the other two houses. The few shillings which were needed in the Boys' Orphan-House, the Lord, however, had previously provided by the little which had come in on December 3 and 4.

Dec. 6. This day our need was again as great as ever, but the deliverance of the Lord was also as manifest as ever. No money had come in, and I knew there would be some needed this morning in all the three houses. That which was required to buy provisions for today, was about 1l.; but there were also coals needed in two houses, and two of the treacle-casks were empty. We gave ourselves, as usual, to prayer. After prayer one of the labourers gave 1l. of the salary which she had received a few days ago; another gave 6s., and 4s. 6d. was taken out of the boxes. Thus we had 1l. 10s. 6d. to divide, and therefore more than was absolutely needed; also one of the labourers had ordered half a ton of coals to be sent to the Boys' Orphan-House, for which he paid himself.

This afternoon I received 100l. from a sister; 50l. for the Orphans, and 50l. for the School--Bible--and Missionary-Fund. This same sister, who earns her bread with her own hands, had given, on October 5, 1837, 50l. towards the Boys' Orphan-House, and gave for the necessities of the poor saints, in August, 1838, 100l. more; for she had been made willing to act out those precious exhortations: "Having food and raiment let us be therewith content." "Sell that ye have, and give alms; provide yourselves bags which wax not old, a treasure in the heavens that faileth not, where no thief approacheth, neither moth corrupteth." "Lay not up for yourselves treasures upon earth, where moth and rust doth corrupt, and where thieves break through and steal: but lay up for yourselves treasures in heaven, where neither moth nor rust doth corrupt, and where thieves do not break through nor steal." Respecting the 50l. which has been given of this sum for the School--Bible--and Missionary-Fund, it is worthy of remark, that we would not order Reference Bibles till we had the means. We had repeatedly prayed respecting this want of Bibles, and particularly again this morning. It had been also much laid on our hearts today, to request that the Lord would enable us to have the Report printed, which we could not do, unless He first sent the means. Lastly, we had also repeatedly asked Him to supply us so largely, if it were His will, as that at the time of the public meetings we might be able to speak again of abundance. For though for some months past the time has been fixed for the public meetings, without any reference to the state of the funds, nevertheless, it might have had the appearance, that we had convened the brethren for the sake of telling them about our poverty, and thus to induce them to give.

Dec. 8, 1838. The Lord closes the third year of this part of the work with blessings. Yesterday was sent 24 yards of flannel, and today were taken out of the box in the Boys' Orphan-House a 5l. note and 3d. Also 2s. was given, and 1l. besides.

Dec. 11, 12, and 13. On the evenings of these three days there were public meetings, at which I gave an account of the Lord's dealing with us in reference to the Orphan-Houses and the other objects of the Scriptural Knowledge Institution. As the work, and particularly that of the Orphan-Houses, was begun for the benefit of the church at large, it appeared well to us, that from time to time it should be publicly stated how the Lord had dealt with us in reference to it; and as on Dec. 9th the third year had been completed, since the commencement of the Orphan work, this seemed to be a suitable time for having these meetings.

Should any one suppose, in reading the plain details of the trials through which we passed during the four months previous to Dec. 9, 1838, respecting the Orphan-Houses, that I have been disappointed as it regards my expectations, as far as the funds are concerned: my answer is, that the reverse is the case. For straits were expected. Long before the trials came, I had more than once stated publicly, that answers to prayer, in the time of need,--the manifestation of the hand of God, stretched out for our help,--was just the very end for which the Institution was established.

I further state, that the Orphans have never lacked any thing. Had I had thousands of pounds in hand, they would have fared no better than they have; for they have always had good nourishing food, the necessary articles of clothing, etc.

It is now (namely on Dec. 10, 1838) four years and nine months since brother Craik and I established the Scriptural Knowledge Institution. The reasons which we had for doing so were, that thus a testimony might be borne that the children of God need not to go to unbelievers to ask them for money; nor require the patronage of the great men of this world in the Lord's work; and that, further, believers generally might be stirred up, to renounce their alliance with the world in the management and promotion of religious objects, and that, lastly, it might be seen, that, without contracting debts, such objects can be carried on.

Painful as it was, and as it still is, to us, to be obliged to differ from so many of our brethren, in these particulars, nevertheless we were called upon to work without them, if we could not conscientiously work with them. May the Lord grant, that the eyes of many of His children may be opened, so that they may seek, in all spiritual things, to be separated from unbelievers, (2 Cor. vi. 14--18), and to do God's work according to God's mind!

I notice briefly the following particulars respecting the first three objects of the Scriptural Knowledge Institution. 1. There is at present (in December, 1838) a Sunday School supported by it, which contains four hundred and sixty-three children. This part of the work calls for particular thanksgiving; for during these last eighteen months the number of the children has been nearly three times as great as it used to be. Five of the scholars have been converted within the last two years, and are now in fellowship with the church, and three of them are teachers in the school. 2. There is in connection with the Institution an Adult-school, in which, since the commencement of the work, above 120 adults have been instructed, and in which at present twelve are taught to read. 3. The Institution has entirely supported, since its commencement, several Day-schools for poor children, and within the last two years six of such: three for boys, and three for girls.--The number of all the children that have had schooling in the Day-schools through the medium of the Institution, since its formation, amounts to 1534; the number of those at present in the six Day. Schools is 342. 4. During the last two years there have been circulated, 1884 copies of the Scriptures in connexion with the Institution, and since the beginning of the work, March 5, 1834, five thousand and seventy-eight copies. 5. For Missionary purposes have been laid out L74. 18s. 4d. 6. The total of the income for the first three objects, during the last two years, was L1129. 13s. 1d. The total of the expenses L1111. 13s. 7 1/2d.

There are, at present, 86 Orphans in the three houses, i. e. 31 in the Girls'-Orphan-House, 31 in the Infant-Orphan-House, and 24 in the Boys'-Orphan-House.

The whole number of Orphans, who have been under our care, from April 11, 1836, to Dec. 9, 1838, amounts to 110.

God's blessing has most manifestly rested upon this part of the work. For, 1. Without any one having been asked for any thing by us, the sum of L2111 5s. 4 1/2d. has been given to us, entirely as the result of prayer to God.

2. Besides this, also, many articles of clothing, furniture, provisions, etc. 3. Without our solicitation three medical gentlemen, (one for each house), have, up to Dec. 9, 1838, kindly given their attendance and medicines gratuitously.

4. The children have been, on the whole, in good health, and many of them have greatly improved as to their health, since they have been with us. 5. Though most of them had been brought up in a very different manner from what one could desire, yet God has constrained them, on the whole, to behave exceedingly well, so much so that it has attracted the attention of all observers. This can be ascribed only to the good hand of God. 6. There are a few among them, respecting whom we have a comfortable assurance that they care about their souls. 7. There is not one of those who have died, of whom we are without hope, as it regards their eternal welfare; but respecting two of them we have especial reason to rejoice. The elder of the two, Harriet Culliford, about twelve years of age when she died, had been for many months wasting away in consumption. She was, almost during the whole time of her illness, completely careless about the things of God; nothing seemed to make any impression upon her, though a well behaved child in other respects. About a fortnight before her departure, she was brought to know the Lord, gave the fullest evidence, that could be given in her circumstances, of a real change of heart, and departed full of joy at the prospect of being with the Lord, though previously she had been very desirous to be restored again. The younger, Leah Culliford, (both of them of a very consumptive family), fell asleep in Jesus on Sept. 11, 1838. She was but little more than eight years of age; but many weeks before her death she gave evidence to those who were placed over her of a change of heart, and of faith in the Lord Jesus Christ.

The total of the income for the Orphans, from Dec. 9, 1836, to Dec. 9, 1838, has amounted to L1341. 4s. 7d. the total of the expenses to L1664. 4s. 0 3/4d. There was two years ago a balance of L373. 4s. 8 1/4d. in hand, and now the balance is L50. 5s. 3d.

Dec. 16. There was a paper anonymously put into the box at Bethesda Chapel, containing 4l. 10s. In the paper was written "For the Rent of the Orphan-Houses, from Dec. 10 to Dec. 31, 1838. 'O taste and see that the Lord is good: blessed is the man that trusteth in Him!" In order that the reader may be able to enter into the value of this donation, I would request him to read over once more, what I wrote under "Sept. 29 of this year." [The individual who gave this 4l. 10s. for the rent of the Orphan-Houses for the first three weeks after the public meetings, at which the matter about the rent, for the instruction of the brethren, was fully stated, continued for three years, up to Dec. 10, 1841, to give regularly, but anonymously, 1l. 10s. a week for the same purpose, which was exactly the sum required every week for the rent of those three houses. Thus the Lord rewarded our faithfulness, in carrying out the light which He had given us. But the chief blessing, resulting from this circumstance, I consider to be this, that several brethren, who earn their bread by the labour of their hands, have learned through this circumstance, that it is the will of the Lord they should lay by their rent weekly. I beseech those brethren who are not pursuing this course, to do so, and they will soon prove by experience the benefit of acting on Scriptural principles even as it regards this life.]

Dec. 17. Today eleven brethren and sisters were proposed for fellowship. The Lord still uses us as instruments. Truly, our labour in the Lord is not in vain!

Dec. 20. As the expenses for the Orphans have been above 47l. within the last six days, and as but little above 13l. has come in, and as the money for printing the Report had to be kept back, in order that we might not be in debt, we were again today very low in funds, though it is but six days since the public meetings. As I knew that tomorrow several pounds would be needed to supply the matrons, I gave myself this morning to prayer. About a quarter of an hour afterwards I received 3l., the payment of a legacy, left by a sister, who fell asleep in Jesus several months since, in Ireland. Besides this I received from the brother, through whom the legacy was paid, 2l. 10s. for the Orphan-Fund. With this 5l. 10s. I hope to be able to meet the expenses of tomorrow.

I observe here that it might have been naturally supposed that every heart would be touched, through what was publicly stated about the remarkable manner in which the Lord had provided for us for nearly 150 days, and that consequently an abundance of means would have come in. To this is to be added, that 50l. 5s. 3d. was in hand on Dec. 10, and that therefore it seemed not likely that we should be in need; and yet, by Dec. 20, we were again so poor, that there was nothing to meet the expenses of the next day, as has just been related. All this came not unawares upon me and my fellow-labourers; for we had been taught to look off from all creature expectations to the living God. It was on this account that, many times in our prayer meetings during November and the beginning of December, we were led to ask the Lord, not to allow us to expect an influx of means because, for the benefit of the Church, our circumstances would be made known at the public meetings. And how kind was it of the Lord to give us prayer about this, and thus to prepare us beforehand; for had we leaned upon natural expectations, we should have been surely disappointed, as only six days after the meetings we were as poor as ever. By the grace of God we are so acquainted with the heart of our Father, that we speak not about these things to excite the compassion of our fellow saints, for we have learned to lean upon God only; but we make known His dealings with us, that others may be led "to taste and see that the Lord is good," and to put their trust in Him.

The sister who left the 3l. for the Orphans, as just alluded to, also left 3l. for the funds of the other objects, 20l. to be divided between brother Craik and me, and 3l. for the poor saints.

Dec. 22. A solemn day. I received today the information from my father that my brother died on October 7th. When I saw him in April this year, he was living in open sin, and in disunion with my father. I cannot learn that his end was different from his life, so that I have no comfort in his death.--Of all the trials that can befall a believer, the death of an unconverted near relative seems to me one of the greatest. "Shall not the judge of all the earth do right?" must be the stay of the believer at such a time, and, by grace, it is my stay now. I know that the Lord is glorified in my brother, whatever his end has been: whether in his last hours, like the thief, on the cross, he was saved, or whether he died in sin and unbelief; yet I do, as to myself, desire from my heart to adore that grace which plucked me as a brand out of the burning, many years ago.--May the Lord make this event a lasting blessing to me, especially in leading me to earnestness in prayer for my father!

Dec. 26. From the 21st to this day several small donations had come in for the Orphans, so that we were supplied as we needed. Today there was ten-pence left, after the day's expenses had been met. One hour after the Lord kindly appeared again. 5l. was sent by Q. Q. This money came, just after I had prayed for means.

Dec. 27. Today came in 2l. 12s. 6d., whereby the Lord has again helped us to meet the probable expenses of tomorrow.

Dec. 28. This evening the Lord kindly sent further help, when we were again destitute of the means of providing for tomorrow. I received 20l. (half for the Orphan-Fund, and half for the other funds), with Ecclesiastes ix. 10: "Whatsoever thy hand findeth to do, do it with thy might; for there is no work, nor device, nor knowledge, nor wisdom, in the grave, whither thou goest."

Dec. 29. A sister, having felt herself particularly stirred up about the Orphans, as she writes, sent this evening 7l. five pounds from herself, and 2l. which had been sent from the EAST INDIES. To the Lord this is to be ascribed, who, in answer to our prayers, makes these impressions on the hearts of His children.

REVIEW OF THE YEAR 1838.

1. As to the church.

68 brethren and sisters we found in fellowship, when brother Craik and I came to Bristol.

458 have been admitted into fellowship since, so that the total number would be

526 had there been no changes. But,

31 have fallen asleep.

28 are under church discipline, which is the total number of all the cases of separation from communion within these six years and seven months.

36 have left Bristol

26 have left us, but are still in Bristol. Only 26 within six years and seven months!

Total 121. There are therefore only 405 at present in fellowship with us. 61 have been added during the last year, of whom 36 have been brought among us to the knowledge of the truth.

II. As to my temporal supplies

The Lord has been pleased to give me during the past year:

1. By the Freewill Offerings through the boxes L151 6s. 8d.

2. By presents in money from believers in and out of Bristol L141 18s. 0d.

3. By money, through family connexion L40 0s. 0d.

4. By presents in clothes, provisions, etc., which were worth to me, at least L12 0s. 0d.

We have been living for six months, half free of rent whereby we have saved at least L5 0s. 0d.

Altogether L350 4s. 8d.

During no period of my life had I such need of means, on account of my own long illness and that of my dear wife, and on account of the many and particular calls for means as during the past year; but also during no period of my life has the Lord so richly supplied me. Truly, it must be manifest to all that I have served a most kind Master, during this year also, and that, even for this life, it is by far the best thing to seek to act according to the mind of the Lord, as to temporal things.

January 1st, 2nd, and 3rd, 1830. We have had three especial church prayer meetings these three days. The year commenced with mercies. In the first hour of the year there came in for the Orphans 2l. 7s., which was given after our usual prayer meeting on December 31, which this time lasted from seven in the evening till after midnight.

Jan. 11. Since December 20, came in several donations for the Orphans, so that we were supplied, before that which we had in hand was quite gone. On the seventh, however, all our money was again expended, when a brother, from the neighbourhood of London, who, is staying here, gave me 10l. Today, when this 10l.

was given out, I received from London 3l. 7s., and 4s. besides. Thus the Lord, as our need is, sends help, and all in answer to prayer, without our asking any one.

Jan. 17. Since the 11th 22 small donations have again come in, by which we have been helped thus far. This afternoon all which was in hand was given for housekeeping, and I was again penniless. The Lord, however, was mindful of this, and in the evening two sovereigns were left anonymously at my house. In the paper was written: "The enclosed are for the use of the Orphan-Houses, from J. H., who thinks he ought to do something for the Institution." J. H. will have in this a proof that the Lord touched his heart to give the money, because there was not a penny in hand for those who are the especial care of Him who is the "Father of the fatherless."

Jan. 20. Ten small donations have come in since the 17th, which have enabled us to provide what was needed for the last three days, and also for today.--For some time past it has appeared to me that the words "Ye have the poor with you always, and whensoever ye will ye may do them good," which the Lord spoke to His disciples, who were themselves very poor, imply that the children of God, as such, have power with God to bring temporal blessings upon poor saints or poor unbelievers, through the instrumentality of prayer. Accordingly I have been led to ask the Lord for means to assist poor saints; and at different times He has stirred up His children to intrust me with sums both large and small, for that especial object; or has, by some means or other, put money at my disposal, which I might so use. In like manner I had been asking again for means a few days since, to be able more extensively to assist the poor saints in communion with us, as just now many of them are not merely tried by the usual temporal difficulties arising from its being winter, but especially from the high price of bread. And now this evening the Lord has given me the answer to my prayer. When I came home from the meeting, I found a brother at my house who offered to give me 10l. a week, for twelve weeks, towards providing the poor saints with coals and needful articles of clothing, but chiefly with bread. [Accordingly this brother sent me two days afterwards 120l.,-- whereby very many, especially poor widows, were greatly assisted, chiefly with flour and bread. This money just lasted till the price of bread was reduced from 9 1/2d. to 7 1/2d. Thus, for several weeks, about 150 quarterns of bread were distributed weekly, besides what was given in flour, coals, and clothes. I have mentioned this circumstance as an encouragement to those who either have little or nothing at all to give to poor persons, and who yet have a desire to give; and to those who have means, but whose means are not adequate to relieve all the demands made upon them. Had we more grace to plead the words of our Lord, above referred to, we should receive far more from Him to meet the necessities around us.]

Jan. 22. A brother formerly an officer in the navy, Who for Jesus' sake has given up his rank and pay, gave three silver table spoons, three silver forks, and two teaspoons, to be sold for the benefit of the Orphans. The produce of them, with 1l. 5s. which has come in besides, enabled us to meet the expenses of today and tomorrow.

Jan. 26. Saturday. The need of the 24th, 25th, and of today was supplied, partly, by the little that had been left on the 23rd; and partly, by five small donations, by 9s. for the children's needlework, and by 12s. which had come in by the sale of two old silk dresses, which had been given for sale. Now, when we were again penniless, 6s. was given me, just after I had been praying for means.

Jan. 28. Monday morning. We are now quite reduced as to means for the Orphans. The little which is in hand has been put by for rent. How the Lord will help us through this day, I know not; but I have faith in God. He will help us, though I know not how. By God's help I purpose not to take a single penny of what is in hand, because it is due for rent.--This morning and afternoon came in from one individual 4s. 6d., and from a sister, who earns her bread by needlework, 1l. There was also 1l. 0s. 10d. taken out of the boxes in the Orphan-Houses, which our need had led us to open. Thus we were helped through the day, and have 1l. left for tomorrow.

Jan. 29. The 1l. which was left helped us through this day; but in the Boys'-Orphan-House were no means to take in bread. In the evening eight small loaves were sent by a sister who could not possibly know our need, and thus we were supplied.

Jan, 30. A little while after I had been in prayer this morning for means for the Orphans, brother T. brought a silver watch and 5s., which had been given last evening. Also, still further, came in this morning five yards of Indian muslin, a zephyr scarf, a muslin dress, and a gold locket, to be sold. About two hours afterwards was sent 1l.

The individual who last evening gave the silver watch and 5s. for the Orphans, called on me today. She is a servant, who in the house of her master found the first part of this Narrative soon after the publication of the first edition, which the Lord used as the means of her conversion. [She fell asleep in Jesus, after having been 36 years in fellowship with us.]

Jan. 31. There came in this morning 2s. 6d. for the Orphans. This, with 1l. in hand, and 10s. which one of the labourers contributed, was sufficient for this day's necessities.

Feb. 1. There is no money in hand for the Orphans. I am waiting on God. Just when Brother T. had come to tell me that the need for this day would be 19s. 6d., one of the labourers in the work came and gave me 1l.

Feb. 2. There are again no means in hand. One of the labourers gave 1l., but I know not whether 1l. will be sufficient for the necessities of this day. This I do know, however, that the Lord will supply us with more, should more be needed. When I met with the brethren and sisters for prayer, one of the labourers gave his watch, under the condition that 1l., which was needed besides that which we had in hand, should be taken from the rent money which had been put by, till it could be replaced; and, if otherwise, that the watch should be sold at the end of the quarter. Just as we had separated, a sovereign was brought to me, which had been sent to my house since I had left it. This was taken instead of the one which had been advanced upon the watch, and thus a speedy answer was granted to our prayers. We have now been brought to the close of one more week.

Feb. 3. Lord's day. A sister sent from her sick bed this evening 2l. for the Orphans, with Ecclesiastes ix. 10. Thus the Lord has supplied our need for tomorrow.

Feb. 4. This afternoon came in two pounds more from the grandmother of two of the Orphans, in answer to prayer, and very seasonably, as the coals in one house are quite out, and nearly so in the other two.

Feb. 5. Today came in 12s., which supplied the necessities of this day.

Feb. 6. Only 10s. 6d. was needed for today, which one of the labourers gave.

Feb. 7. This day has been one of the most remarkable days as it regards the Funds. There was no money in hand, I was waiting upon God. I had asked him repeatedly, but no supplies came. Brother T. called between 11 and 12 o'clock, to tell me that about 1l. 2s. would be needed, to take in bread for the three houses, and to meet the other expenses; but we had only 2s. 9d., which yesterday had been taken out of the boxes in the Orphan-Houses. He went to Clifton to make arrangements for the reception of the three orphans of our sister Loader, who fell asleep on the 4th; for though we have no funds in hand, the work goes on, and our confidence is not diminished. I therefore requested him to call on his way back from Clifton, to see whether the Lord might have sent any money in the mean time. When he came I had received nothing, but one of the labourers, having 5s. of his own, gave it. It was now four o'clock. I knew not how the sisters had got through the day. Just before I went out to preach, 5s. was brought to my house, which I took as a token for good. I had been asking the Lord for a passage of the Word to speak from this evening, and at last was directed to Matt. vi. 19-34, a subject most applicable to our circumstances. After the meeting was over, I went to the Girls'-Orphan-House, to meet with the brethren for prayer, and to give the 5s. which I had received, and to see what could be done. When I arrived there, I found that a box had come for me from Barnstaple. The carriage was paid, else there would have been no money to pay for it. (See how the Lord's hand is in the smallest matters!) The box was opened, and it contained, in a letter from a sister, 10l., of which 8l. was for the Orphans, and 2l. for the Bible Fund; from brethren at Barnstaple, 2l. 11s. 2d.; and from another brother 5s. Besides this, there were in the box 4 yards of merino, 3 pairs of new shoes, 2 pairs of new socks: also six books for sale. Likewise a gold pencil-case, 2 gold rings, 2 gold drops of ear-rings, a necklace, and a silver pencil-case. On inquiry, how the sisters had been carried through the day, I found it thus: everything was in the houses which was needed for dinner. After dinner a lady from Thornbury came and bought one of my Narratives and one of the Reports, and gave 3s. besides. About five minutes afterwards the baker came to the Boys'-Orphan-House. The matron of the Girls'-Orphan-House seeing him, went immediately with the 6s. 6d. which she had just received, (to prevent his being sent away, as there was no money in hand at the Boys'-Orphan-House,) and bought bread to the amount of 4s. 6d. The two remaining shillings, with the little which was in hand, served to buy bread for the Girls'-Orphan-House. By the donations sent in the box, I was enabled to give a rich supply to the matrons before the close of the day.

How sweet to see our Father thus caring for us! To a person who has spiritual eyes, what a proof is one such day of the most particular providence of God! And we have had many such days.

Feb. 8. Today the Lord sent still further help, which is remarkable for two reasons in particular. First, we had decided yesterday upon receiving the three little Loaders, though we were so low as to funds. Thus the Lord sent means on their behalf. Secondly, we were brought so low yesterday, and our faith was so much tried, in order that now again the abundance of supplies out of our loving Father's hand, might be so much the sweeter. A sister in the neighbourhood of London sent today in money 1l. 5s., and the following articles for sale; 3 purses, 1 mourning brooch, 1 amber ditto, 1 amethyst stud, 1 cameo ditto, I pair of coral ear rings, 1 coral cross, 1 ring set with a diamond and six rubies, 1 ditto pearl and garnet, 1 ditto garnet, 1 ruby cross, 4 necklaces, and 148 pamphlets and tracts. Also several articles of clothing for the children.

Feb. 13. Since the 8th, five donations, amounting to 9l. 9s., had come in. This afternoon I paid out the last money which we had in hand, and in giving it to brother T. said, we have now again to look to the Lord for further supplies. This evening 5l. was given to me, which had come in under the folio wing circumstances:--

A gentleman and lady visited the Orphan-Houses, and met at the Boys'-Orphan-House two ladies who were likewise visiting. One of the ladies said to the matron of the Boys'-Orphan-House: "Of course, you cannot carry on these institutions without a good stock of funds." The gentleman, turning to the matron, said, "Have you a good stock?" She replied: "Our funds are deposited in a bank which cannot break." The tears came into the eyes of the inquiring lady. The gentleman, on leaving, gave to the master of the boys 5l., which came in when I had not a penny in hand.

Feb. 16. Yesterday came in 17s. 6d. for the Orphans, which, with what was taken out of the boxes today, helped us through; and thus we have been brought to the close of one more week.

March 5. Up to this day, since Feb. 16, the supplies for the Orphans have come in so seasonably, that we were able comfortably to meet all the demands. Today, however, I knew that there would be again several pounds required, as, besides the daily provisions, there were coals needed, the treacle-casks in two houses were empty, and there was but 5s. in hand. I gave myself therefore to prayer this morning. WHILST I WAS IN PRAYER, Q. Q. sent a cheque for 7l. 10s. Thus the Lord has again most seasonably helped us out of our difficulty. There came in still further this day, 1l. 19s. 2d., by the sale of some articles, which had been given for the benefit of the Orphans.

March 6. For some time past the minds of several brethren among us, as well as that of brother Craik and my own, had been much exercised respecting certain questions connected with points of church order and discipline, on account of which brother Craik and I were absent from Bristol during the last two weeks, to give ourselves to prayer and consideration respecting those points. Since our return we have had, these last three evenings, meetings with the saints, before whom we stated the result to which we had been led, after prayer and examination of the Scriptures. The following is an abstract of what was stated at those meetings, which I give here, as this matter forms an important period in my experience about church matters; but the abstract will be of little use, except the reader consider carefully the passages to which reference is made.

I.--QUESTIONS RESPECTING THE ELDERSHIP.

(1) How does it appear to be the mind of God, that, in every Church, there should be recognized Elders?

Ans. From the following passages compared together, Matth. xxiv. 45, Luke xii. 42. From these passages we learn that some are set by the Lord Himself in the office of Rulers and Teachers, and that this office (in spite of the fallen state of the Church) should be in being even down to the close of the present dispensation. Accordingly, we find from Acts xiv. 23, xx. 17, Tit. i. 5, and 1 Pet. v. 1, that soon after the saints had been converted, and had associated together in a Church character, Elders were appointed to take the rule over them and to fulfil the office of under-shepherds.

This must not be understood as implying, that, when believers are associated in Church fellowship, they ought to elect Elders according to their own will, whether the Lord may have qualified persons or not; but rather that such should wait upon God, that He Himself would be pleased to raise up such as may be qualified for teaching and ruling in His church.

(2) How do such come into office?

Ans. By the appointment of the Holy Ghost, Acts xx. 28.

(3) How may this appointment be made known to the individuals called to the office, and to those amongst whom they may be called to labour?

Ans. By the secret call of the Spirit, 1 Tim. iii. 1, confirmed by the possession of the requisite qualifications, 1 Tim. iii. 2-7, Tit. i. 6-9, and by the Lord's blessing resting upon their labours, 1 Cor. ix. 2.

In 1 Cor. ix. 2, Paul condescends to the weakness of some, who were in danger of being led away by those factious persons who questioned his authority. As an Apostle--appointed by the express word of the Lord--he needed not such outward confirmation. But if he used his success as an argument in confirmation of his call, how much more may ordinary servants of the Lord Jesus employ such an argument, seeing that the way, in which they are called for the work, is such as to require some outward confirmation.

(4) Is it incumbent upon the saints to acknowledge such and to submit to them in the Lord?

Ans. Yes. See 1 Cor. xvi. 15, 16, 1 Thess. v. 12, 13, Heb. xiii. 7, 17, and 1 Tim. v. 17. In these passages obedience to pastoral authority is clearly enjoined.

II.--Ought matters of discipline to be finally settled by the Elders in private, or in the presence of the Church, and as the act of the whole body?

Ans. (1) Such matters are to be finally settled in the presence of the Church. This appears from Matth. xviii. 17, 1 Cor. v. 4, 5, 2 Cor. ii. 6-8, 1 Tim. v. 20. (2) Such matters are to be finally settled as the act of the whole body, Matth. xviii. 17, 18. In this passage the act of exclusion is spoken of as the act of the whole body. 1 Cor. v. 4, 5, 7, 12, 13. In this passage Paul gives the direction, respecting the exercise of discipline, in such a way as to render the whole body responsible: verse 7, "Purge out the old leaven, that ye maybe a new lump;" and verse 13, "Therefore put away from among yourselves that wicked person." From 2 Cor. ii. 6-8, we learn that the act of exclusion was not the act of the Elders only, but of the Church. "Sufficient to such a man is this punishment (rather, public censure) which was inflicted of many." From verse 8 we learn that the act of restoration was to be a public act of the brethren: "Wherefore I beseech you that ye would confirm (rather ratify by a public act) your love towards him."

As to the reception of brethren into fellowship, this is an act of simple obedience to the Lord, both on the part of the Elders and the whole Church. We are bound and privileged to receive all those who make a credible profession of faith in Christ, according to that Scripture, "Receive ye one another, as Christ also received us, to the glory of God." Rom. xv. 7.

59

III.--When should Church acts (such as acts of reception, restoration, exclusion, &c.) be attended to?

Ans. It cannot be expressly proved from Scripture, whether such acts were attended to at the meeting for the breaking of bread, or at any other meeting; therefore this is a point on which, if different churches differ, mutual forbearance ought to be exercised. The way in which such matters have hitherto been managed amongst us has been by the Church coming together on a week-evening. Before we came to Bristol we had been accustomed to this mode, and, finding nothing in Scripture against it, we continued the practice. But, after prayer, and more careful consideration of this point, it has appeared well to us that such acts should be attended to on the Lord's days, when the saints meet together for the breaking of bread. We have been induced to make this alteration by the following reasons:--

(1) This latter mode prevents matters from being delayed. There not being a sufficiency of matter for a meeting on purpose every week, it has sometimes happened, that, what would better have been stated to the Church at once, has been kept back from the body for some weeks. Now, it is important that what concerns the whole Church, should be made known as soon as possible to those who are in fellowship, that they may act accordingly. Delay, moreover, seems inconsistent with the pilgrim-character of the people of God.

(2) More believers can be present on the Lord's days than can attend on week evenings. The importance of this reason will appear from considering how everything which concerns the Church should be known to as many as possible. For how can the saints pray for those who may have to be excluded,--how can they sympathize in cases of peculiar trial,--and how can they rejoice and give thanks on account of those who may be received or restored, unless they are made acquainted with the facts connected with such cases?

(3) A testimony is thus given that all who break bread are Church members. By attending to Church acts in the meeting for breaking of bread, we show that we make no difference between receiving into fellowship at the Lord's supper, and into Church membership; but that the individual who is admitted to the Lord's table is therewith also received to all the privileges, trials, and responsibilities of Church membership.

(4) There is a peculiar propriety in acts of reception, restoration and exclusion being attended to when the saints meet together for the breaking of bread, as, in that ordinance especially, we show forth our fellowship with each other.

Objections answered.

(1) This alteration has the appearance of changeableness.

Reply. Such an objection would apply to any case in which increased light led to any improvement, and is, therefore, not to be regarded. It would be an evil thing if there were any change respecting the foundation truths of the Gospel; but the point in question is only a matter of Church order.

(2) More time may thus be required than it would be well to give to such a purpose on the Lord's day.

Reply. As, according to this plan, Church business will be attended to every Lord's day, it is more than probable that the meetings will be thereby prolonged for a few minutes only; but should circumstance required it, a special meeting may still be appointed during the week, for all who break bread with us. This, however, would only be needful, provided the matters to be brought before the brethren were to require more time than could be given to them at the breaking of bread.

N.B. (1) Should any persons be present who do not break bread with us, they may be requested to withdraw, whenever such points require to be stated, as it would not be well to speak of in the presence of unbelievers.

(2) As there are two places in which the saints meet for the breaking of bread, the matters connected with Church acts must be brought out at each place.

IV.--QUESTIONS RELATIVE TO THE LORD'S SUPPER.

(1) How frequently ought the breaking of bread to be attended to?

Ans. Although we have no express command respecting the frequency of its observance, yet the example of the apostles and of the first disciples would lead us to observe this ordinance every Lord's day. Acts xx. 7.

(2) What ought to be the character of the meeting at which the saints are assembled for the breaking of bread?

Ans. As in this ordinance we show forth our common participation in all the benefits of our Lord's death, and our union to Him and to each other (1 Cor. x. 16, 17,) opportunity ought to be given for the exercise of the gifts of teaching or exhortation, and communion in prayer and praise. Rom. xii. 4--8, Eph. iv. 11--16. The manifestation of our common participation in each other's gifts cannot be fully given at such meetings, if the whole meeting is, necessarily, conducted by one individual. This mode of meeting does not however take off from those, who have the gifts of teaching or exhortation, the responsibility of edifying the church, as opportunity may be offered.

(3) Is it desirable that the bread should be broken at the Lord's Supper by one of the Elders, or should each individual of the body break it for himself?

Ans. Neither way can be so decidedly proved from Scripture, that we are warranted in objecting to the other as positively unscriptural, yet--

(1) The letter of Scripture seems rather in favour of its being done by each brother and sister, 1 Cor. x. 16, 17. "The bread which we break."

(2) Its being done by each of the disciples, is more fitted to express that we all, by our sins, have broken the body of our Lord.

(3) By attending to the ordinance in this way, we manifest our freedom from the common error that the Lord's supper must be administered by some particular individual, possessed of what is called a ministerial character, instead of being an act of social worship and obedience.

[Before brother Craik and I left Bristol for the consideration of the above points, things wore a gloomy appearance. A separation in the church seemed to be unavoidable. But God had mercy, and pitied us. He was pleased to give us not merely increased light, but showed us also how to act, and gave us a measure of wisdom, grace and spiritual courage for acting. The clouds were dispelled, and peace was restored in the church.]

While I was away from Bristol, Samuel Loader, a little orphan boy, died, after a fortnight's residence in the house, and only three weeks after his mother's death. The brethren in the Boys-Orphan-House consider him to have died in the faith.

March 16. Saturday. By the good hand of the Lord we are brought to the close of one more week. I have been able to meet all the current expenses for the Orphans, and to pay, besides this, 10l. for salaries. Thus a part of what has been due for several weeks to my dear fellow-labourers is defrayed. I have especially prayed within the last ten days that the Lord would be pleased to give me the means for this. 2s. 8 1/2d. I have left.

March 18. Monday. Last evening 5l. came in with Eccles. ix. 10. Thus we were again enabled to supply all the necessities of this day.

Pause a few moments, dear reader! Consider how seasonably the Lord sends the supplies! Not once does He forget us! Not once is our need only half supplied! Not once do His supplies come too late! Dear reader, if you have not the like experience of the Lord's watchful care, Oh taste and see that the Lord is good!

March 20. The need of the 18th and 19th was supplied by the 5l. which had come in on the 18th. Today we were again poor and needy, therefore the Lord thought on us, and sent us 3l. l6s. 1 1/2d.

March 22. Some trinkets which had been given, and 12s. which was in hand, supplied the need of today. Yesterday were sent six sacks of potatoes. We were not able to lay in a stock last autumn (as we had done the two previous autumns) on account of want of means, but in no previous year have we had so many sent.

March 23. Today I received a letter from brother T., who is on account of his health in Devonshire, to inform me that a heavy gold chain, a ring set with ten brilliants, a pair of gold bracelets, and 2l. have been given to him. He gave a Report to a brother, who, having read it, was thereby stirred up to prayer, and knowing that his believing sister possessed these trinkets, he asked the Lord to incline her heart to give them up for the benefit of our Orphans, which she soon after did. By means of these donations I am able both to meet the remaining expenses of this week, and also to pay 15l., which still remains due on account of the salaries. My fellow-labourers not only never ask me for any thing, but are willing to part with money, or any thing else in the hour of need; nevertheless, I had asked the Lord about this point frequently, and He has now given me my request, whereof I am glad. I received also this afternoon 5l. 10s., besides a number of things to be disposed of for the Orphans.

March 24. The Lord has again kindly opened His liberal hand today, and given us 6l. 10s. Thus we have wherewith to meet the necessities of tomorrow in the Orphan-Houses.

From March 24 to April 7, came in about sixty small donations. This, with the produce of the sale of the trinkets, supplied all our need for the Orphans.

April 7. Our funds were now again spent, except 15s., though three days ago above 30l. had come in; therefore the Lord has sent in again this day several contributions, altogether 6l. 5s.

April 8. The money which came in yesterday was sent off today for housekeeping in the three different houses, and when I was now again left penniless, there came in 2l. 6s. 10d.

April 9. The 2l. 6s. 10d. was given out today for housekeeping, and I am once more penniless.--A few hours after I had written this, there was given to me by a brother 2l. 10s. When I received this money, I was at the same time informed of the death of one of our sisters, a widow, whose child we can receive.

April 10. Today was sent anonymously from the country 5l. In the evening I received still further 1l. l6s. 6d.

April 11. It is three years today since the first Orphans were received. Good indeed has the Lord been to us during these three years! We have lacked nothing! Again He has sent this day, in a remarkable manner, 5l., with the following letter, addressed to a brother:

"My dear Friend, enclosed are 5l. for the Orphan-Asylum, the history of which is rather interesting. We have a servant who lived some years ago as kitchen-maid in a noble family (i. e. the master a wealthy member of Parliament, the mistress an Earl's daughter.) No perquisites were allowed; but the individual in question acted on the same principle as her fellow-servants, and sold kitchen-stuff for her own benefit, which she thinks might amount to 4l.; and therefore she believes that 5l. would fully repay principal and interest. This money is of course due to her former master and mistress, with whom I have had several interviews on the subject. They were disposed that the money should be given to some charity; and in consequence of reading one of the Reports you kindly sent me, the young woman had a great desire that her own repentance might yield fruit to that work of faith and love. Her wishes have been sanctioned by her former mistress. It is rather remarkable that our truly Christian servant had been converted a year and a half, before this individual sin, calling for pecuniary restitution, had come into her remembrance."

April 13. I conversed with another of the Orphans, who seems to have been truly converted, and who has walked consistently for many months. Tomorrow she will be united with the saints in communion. She will be the third in fellowship with us, and several have died in the faith. How has the Lord owned the work, even in this respect!

April 14. Today 5l. 0s. 8d. came in for the Orphans, 1l. of which is one of the most remarkable gifts that we have ever had. A poor brother, with a large family, and small wages (there are eight in the family, and he had 15s. wages till lately, when they were raised to 18s.) put by this money by little and little of what was given him by his master for beer. This brother, who was converted about five years ago, was before that time a notorious drunkard.

April 30. Today our dear young brother, John Short, only a little more than 14 years old, fell asleep, after having been for several years ill. He had been for several years converted. He was one of our Sunday-School children before his illness. When, many months since, he lost one of his limbs by amputation, he glorified the Lord not merely by the way in which he sustained the severe suffering attending the operation, but also by confessing the Lord, as his strength, in the hour of trial. He was a sweet youth!

July 2. Today was given me, when there was not one shilling in hand, 50l. for the School--Bible--and Missionary-Fund.

July 15. Monday. Today 2l. 7s. 3d. was needed for the Orphans, but we had nothing. How to obtain the means for a dinner, and for what else was needed, I knew not. My heart was perfectly at peace, and unusually sure of help, though I knew not in the least whence it was to come. Before brother T. came, I received a letter from India, written in May, with an order for 50l. for the Orphans. I had said last Saturday to brother T., that it would be desirable to have 50l., as the salaries of all my fellow-labourers are due, the three treacle-casks empty, all the provision stores exhausted, several articles of clothing needed, and worsted for the boys to go on with their knitting. Now the Lord has sent exactly 50l. Moreover this money comes very seasonably, as in three days I shall have to leave Bristol for some days, and can now go comfortably, as it regards leaving means behind.

[In the afternoon of this same day I met at a brother's house with several believers, when a sister said that she had often thought about the care and burden I must have on my mind, as it regards obtaining the necessary supplies for so many persons. As this may not be a solitary instance, I would state, that, by the grace of God, this is no cause of anxiety to me. The children I have years ago cast upon the Lord. The whole work is His, and it becomes me to be without carefulness. In whatever points I am lacking, in this point I am able, by the grace of God, to roll the burden upon my heavenly Father. Though now (July 1845) for about seven years our funds have been so exhausted, that it has been comparatively a rare case that there have been means in hand to meet the necessities of the Orphans for three days together; yet have I been only once tried in spirit, and that was on Sept. 18, 1838, when for the first time the Lord seemed not to regard our prayer. But when He did send help at that time, and I saw that it was only for the trial of our faith, and not because He had forsaken the work that we were brought so low, my soul was so strengthened and encouraged, that I have not only not been allowed to distrust the Lord since that time, but I have not even been cast down when in the deepest poverty. Nevertheless, in this respect also am I now, as much as ever, dependant on the Lord; and I earnestly beseech for myself and my fellow-labourers the prayers of all those, to whom the glory of God is dear. How great would be the dishonour to the name of God, if we, who have so publicly made our boast in Him, should so fall as to act in these very points as the world does! Help us then, brethren, with your prayers, that we may trust in God to the end. We can expect nothing but that our faith will yet be tried, and it may be more than ever; and we shall fall, if the Lord does not uphold us.]

July 16 and 17. These two days we have had two especial prayer meetings, to commend to the Lord five German brethren who for some weeks have been sojourning among us, and who purpose to leave tomorrow for Liverpool, to sail from thence to the East Indies.

July 18. I left this morning with the German brethren, to accompany them to Liverpool.

July 21. Liverpool. This afternoon I preached in the open air on the docks. Truly, it must be a sweet privilege to be permitted frequently to proclaim the glad tidings of the Gospel in the open air, which the Lord does not bestow upon me, as, under ordinary circumstances, I have no strength for this work.--The people were attentive. There was but one who mocked.

July 22. Preached again out of doors.

July 23. I accompanied the five brethren on board this afternoon.

July 27. Today I had another remarkable proof of the importance of the children of God opening their hearts to each other, especially when they are getting into a cold state, or are under the power of a certain sin, or are in especial difficulty. An individual called on me, who I trust is a brother, with whom I had conversed once before, but felt uncomfortable respecting him. When he called again today, it appeared to me that there was something upon his heart, which, if I could but know, I might be instrumental in benefiting him. I pressed him affectionately to open his heart, assuring him at the same time that the matter which he might speak of should remain in my own bosom. At last I succeeded. [The result of this conversation was, that the advice which I gave him, led him, after three days, to leave for America, where he ought to have been, instead of being in England; and if he has followed my advice, in one other point, the matter which for years had burdened his conscience, and which, no doubt had been the means of keeping him in a low spiritual state, will have no more power over him. Should this fall into the hands of any children of God who have a particular trial or burden, or a guilty conscience, on account of a particular thing, or a besetting sin, etc., on account of which it would be beneficial to open their hearts to another child of God, in whose love, spiritual judgment, etc., they have confidence, I would advise them to do so. I know from my own experience, how often the snare of the devil has been broken, when under the power of sin; how often the heart has been comforted, when nigh to be overwhelmed; how often advice, under great perplexity, has been obtained,--by opening my heart to a brother in whom I had confidence. We are children of the same family, and ought therefore to be helpers one of another.]

Aug. 3. L3. 5s. was required to meet the necessities of the Orphan-Houses this day. The Lord enabled us to meet this demand, partly, by the sale of some Indian muslin, which had been given some months since, but which was only now disposed of; partly, by a few small donations; and partly, by what one of the labourers added of his own. [We have often found that the money for articles, which were put out to be sold, has come in most seasonably. At this time it happened so that a brother, into whose hands the muslin had been put, felt himself stirred up to go and ask the individual who had it for sale whether she had disposed of it. This brother knew nothing about our need at that time.]

Aug. 5. Monday. On Saturday and yesterday morning I had repeatedly asked the Lord to send us help, as there was not a penny in hand for the need of today. Yesterday morning a brother gave me two sovereigns, and in the evening I received two more. Besides this, there was 4l. 10s. anonymously given for three weeks' rent for the Orphan-Houses, also 10s. by a brother, and 9s. came in for needlework of the children; so that altogether 9l. 9s. came in yesterday.

This evening I took tea with a sister who purposes to leave Bristol tomorrow for Van Diemen's Land. [For the comfort of any saints, who may be similarly situated, I mention the following circumstance. The son of this sister was transported many years since. In the course of time he obtained a business of his own in Van Diemen's Land, and wished his mother to come to him. The mother went, and had, in answer to the prayers of the saints, a prosperous voyage. When she arrived, she found her son truly converted. What a joy for the long and deeply afflicted mother! What remarkable means the Lord uses to bestow blessings! Moreover, to mark that the Lord had sent her to her son, she found that a month before her arrival his wife had died, and that she therefore reached him just at the right time, both on account of his children and his business.]

Aug. 7. Today again about 3l. was needed for housekeeping at the Orphan-Houses, which the Lord had sent in since the day before yesterday, so that we were able to meet all the demands.

Aug. 8. Today 1l. 3s. was needed, but only 3s. had come in. The deficiency was supplied by one of the labourers giving a sovereign of his own. Though there is no money in hand, yet are we so little discouraged, that we have received today one orphan boy, and have given notice for the admission of six other children, which will bring the number up to 98 altogether.

Aug. 9. Only 10s. had come in since yesterday, and as 30s. were needed, one of the labourers gave a sovereign.

Aug. 10. Saturday. The need of today is 2l. 10s. but only 10s, has been given since yesterday. One of the labourers, having 2l., gave it, and thus our need was supplied. ʼ

Aug. 12. Monday. The Lord has again kindly sent 11l. Of this sum 10l. came in from Q. Q., when again there was not one penny in hand. We have now supplies for about four days.

Aug. 14. Today was very seasonably sent a whole piece of calico and a piece of print.

Aug. 16. All our money is now again gone. Today 1l. 3s. was needed, but only 3s. was in hand. One of the labourers was able to add a sovereign, and thus we were helped.

Aug. 17. Saturday. 5l. was needed today, but only 7s. 6d. had come in. The remaining 2l. 12s. 6d. one of the labourers gave. Thus we were helped to the close of another week.

Aug. 19. Monday. This has been again a day in which our faith has been particularly tried; but even this day we have not been confounded. Not one penny was in hand when the day began. We had therefore now, for more than one hundred persons, again to look to the Lord. But this I must say, to the praise of the Lord, my soul was perfectly at peace. I meant to have gone very early to the Orphan-Houses to meet with my fellow-labourers for prayer; but, as one person after the other called upon me, I was kept from it the whole morning. When brother T. called upon me between 12 and 1 o'clock for money, I had none to give. In the afternoon at four I was able to meet with the brethren and sisters. When I came to the Girls'-Orphan-House, I found that one of those children, for the reception of whom we had given notice, had been brought from Bath, and with him was sent 1l. 5s. After the meeting was over, one of the labourers gave 10s. By means of this 1l. 15s. we were able for this day also to provide every thing needful.

Aug. 20. When we met together this morning for prayer, only one shilling had come in since yesterday, and 2l. at least was needed to meet the expenses of this day. After prayer, one of the labourers gave 10s., and 1s. 1 1/2d. was taken out of one of the boxes. This 12s. 1 1/2d. was divided to meet the momentary need. About an hour afterwards, 1l. 14s. came in, being the payment, in part, of articles which had been sold several months since.

Aug. 21. Nothing had come in since yesterday. 13s. would have been needed to have taken in the usual quantity of bread. After we had prayed, the same labourer who had contributed yesterday and the day before, gave today 5s. more. This helped us to buy milk; but in one of the houses the usual quantity of bread could not be taken in. I have further to notice respecting this time of trial, that I had purposed to have gone yesterday to Bath, to meet today and tomorrow with several brethren, who are met there from various parts of the country, to unite in prayer for the present spiritual necessities of the church at large. However, on account of our present need in the Orphan-Houses, I could not go yesterday, as I did not think it right to let my fellow-labourers bear the trial alone. Today also I have been kept here, as our poverty is greater than ever. Yet (the Lord be praised!) neither have the children in the least lacked this day, nor has my mind been in any degree disturbed. My fellow-labourers also seem quite in peace. We are waiting for deliverance, and we are sure that the Lord, in His own time, will send it.

Aug. 22. In my morning walk, when I was reminding the Lord of our need, I felt assured that He would send help this day. My assurance sprang from our need; for there seemed no way to get through the day, without help being sent. After breakfast I considered whether there was any thing which might be turned into money for the dear children. Among other things, there came under my hands a number of religious pamphlets which had been given for the benefit of the Orphans; but all seemed not nearly enough, to meet the necessities of the day, In this our deep poverty, after I had gathered together the few things for sale, a sister, who earns her bread by the labour of her hands, brought 82l. This sister had seen it to be binding upon believers in our Lord Jesus to act out His commandments: "Sell that ye have (sell your possessions) and give alms," Luke xii. 33; and "Lay not up for yourselves treasures upon earth," Matt. vi. 19. Accordingly she had drawn her money out of the bank and stocks, being 250l., and had brought it to me at three different times for the benefit of the Orphans, the Bible--Missionary--and School-Fund, and the poor saints, About two months ago she brought me 100l. more, being the produce of some other possession which she had sold, the half of which was to be used for the School--Bible-and Missionary Fund; and the other half for the poor saints. This 82l. which she had brought today, is the produce of the sale of her last earthly possession.--[At the time I am preparing the seventh edition for the press, more than twenty-nine years have passed away, and this sister has never expressed the least regret as to the step she took, but goes on, quietly labouring with her hands, to earn her bread.]--But even now, when this money was given, I left it in the hands of the Lord, whether any part of it should be applied for the Orphans. I asked the sister, therefore, whether she wished the money to be spent in any particular way, as she had expressed her wish about the former sums. This time she left it with me, to lay out the money as I thought best. I took, therefore, half of it for the Orphans, and half for the other objects of the Scriptural Knowledge Institution. I have thus been enabled to come to Bath, (after I had sent a more than usual supply to the matrons), to meet, at least for the remaining time, with the brethren who are assembled here for prayer. Before the day is over, I have received 10l. more, while at Bath, from one of the brethren who are assembled here; so that our deep poverty, in the morning, has been turned into a comparative abundance.

Aug. 23. The Lord has sent still further supplies. Another of the brethren gave me this morning 1l., and a third, with whom I drove back to Bristol, 5l.

From Aug. 25 to Sept. 1, there came in above 17l. more.

Sept. 4. I have been led to pray whether it is the Lord's will that I should leave Bristol for a season, as I have for the last fortnight been suffering from indigestion, by which my whole system is weakened, and thus the nerves of my head are more than usually affected. There are, however, two hindrances in the way, want of means for the Orphans, and want of means for my own personal expenses.--Today I have received a cheque from Q. Q. for 7l. 10s. for the Orphans, which came, therefore, very seasonably. Also 4l. besides has came in since the day before yesterday.

Sept. 5. Today a sister sent me 5l. for myself, to be used for the benefit of my health. She had heard that my health is again failing. I do not lay by money for such purposes; but whenever I really need means, whether for myself or others, the Lord sends them, in answer to prayer; for He had in this case again given me prayer respecting means for myself and for the Orphans, that my way might be made plain as to leaving Bristol for a season.

Sept. 6. My body is now so weak, and my head again so affected in consequence of it, and I have found it needful to give up the work at once. I left today for Trowbridge, for three days, intending afterwards to go with my wife into Devonshire, if the Lord permit.

Sept. 7. Trowbridge. This has been a very good day. I have had much communion with the Lord. How kind to take me from the work at Bristol for a season, to give me more communion with Himself. I remembered the Lord's especial goodness to me in this place, at the commencement of last year. How kind has He also been since! I prayed much for myself, for the Church at large, for the saints here and in Bristol, for my unconverted relatives, for my dear wife, and that the Lord would supply my own temporal necessities and those of the Orphans:--and I know that He has heard me.--I am surrounded with kind friends in the dear saints, under whose roof I am, and feel quite at home. My room is far better than I need; yet an easy chair, in this my weak state of body, to kneel before in prayer, would have added to my comfort. In the afternoon, without having given a hint about it, I found an easy chair put into my room. I was struck with the kindness, the especial kindness of my heavenly Father, in being mindful of the smallest wants and comforts of His child.-- Having had more prayer than usual, I found that my intercourse with the saints at tea was with unction, and more than usually profitable. But this very fact reminds me of my sad deficiencies, and of my great lack of real fervency of spirit. May the Lord carry on His work with power in my soul! Today I had 1l. given to me, half for the Orphans, and half for the other funds. Thus the Lord has begun to answer my prayers; for I expect far more.

Sept. 8. Lord's day. I assembled with a few saints at Trowbridge, and spoke to them in the morning and evening with much assistance. The afternoon I spent at home over the Word and in prayer. God has evidently blessed the Word. He had a purpose in sending me here, both for blessing to myself and to others.

Sept. 9. This morning I conversed with a poor aged sister in the Lord, who for 47 years has been a believer, but who, from want of settling by the written Word only, whether she is a believer or not, has often had doubts about her state before God. However, I brought the Scriptures only before her. [My pressing the Scriptures alone upon her heart, was made such a blessing, that I hear she has not doubted in the same way since.] This aged sister told me she often prays for the Orphans, and for the continuance of means. How many helpers has the Christian in the conflict; yet all are strengthened by ONE who is ALWAYS for us!

This evening I returned to Bristol, to go from hence tomorrow to Exeter, if the Lord permit, on account of my health. I had been earnestly asking the Lord, while I was staying at Trowbridge, that He would be pleased to send in supplies for the Orphans, before I go into Devonshire, and I had the fullest assurance that means would come in before I left Bristol. I therefore asked my wife, on my return, how much had come in, and found that it was only 8l. 9s. 7 3/4d. This was not nearly as much as I had expected, and would not answer the end for which I had particularly asked means, i. e. that I might be able to leave enough for several days. My reply therefore was, according to the faith given to me, and judging from the earnestness and confidence of my prayer, that the Lord would send more before I left. About an hour after, brother Craik brought me 10l., which he had received this evening with Ecclesiastes ix. 10, and also a letter from a brother at Ilfracombe, in which the arrival of a large box, full of articles, to be sold for the benefit of the Orphans, is announced. Thus the Lord has dealt with me according to my faith.

Sept. 10. This morning before I left Bristol came in still further 11. 16s. 7d., so that I had about 20l. to leave behind for the present need. I found also, on opening the box which has arrived, 65 books, a brace of valuable pistols, and a great many articles of East India linen. How kind of the Lord to send these supplies just now!

After my departure from Bristol I continued to help my fellow-labourers by my prayers. I had the fullest assurance that the Lord would help them, and my hope was not ashamed, as will appear from the following part of the journal.--In the evening of Sept. 10th, we arrived in Exeter, where we were lodged by a brother, who on the following day left for Plymouth. The love of this brother constrained us to remain for five days at his house, though he was absent, leaving us all the house with a sister, as a servant, to ourselves. Though at another time I should have preferred the opportunity of having intercourse with this brother, yet now, in this my weak state of body, the being left alone was the very thing which suited me. I could not but trace the kind hand of God in this circumstance. I was able to speak twice publicly while in Exeter. I rejoiced at what I saw there of the work of God. This city was in the year 1830 especially laid on my heart, when I used frequently to preach there; but then there was a great spiritual deadness.

From Sept. 16th to Sept. 28th we were at Teignmouth my former field of labour. I had not seen the brethren, among whom I used to labour, since May, 1833. The Lord gave me strength, many times to minister in the Word among them, during the time of my stay there. At Teignmouth also, I had, in some respects, reason to be glad, particularly in that I saw some of those truths practised, and that more fully and intelligently, which, though in much weakness and indistinctly, I had sought to set forth whilst labouring there. At Teignmouth also, as well as in Exeter, the saints showed us much love. A brother and sister lodged us during the whole of our stay. May the Lord reward them for their love!--While I was at Teignmouth I received on Sept. 18th, the following letter from brother T., in reference to the work in Bristol:--

Bristol, Sept. 16, 1839.

My dear Brother, I have delayed writing until now, that, as I hoped, I might have additional news to tell you after the Lord's day. And now that my hope has been made good, I rejoice to do so. The Lord has dealt most graciously with us since your departure. The children, brother B. and the sisters are well, and the wants of the Orphans have been abundantly supplied. There has come in altogether 24l. 8s. 6d., &c.

On Sept. 24th, I received another letter from brother T., dated Bristol, Sept. 23rd, in which he writes: "It rejoices me that I have still nothing but the goodness of the Lord to tell you of. That little word 'Ebenezer' is at once our encouragement and our daily song, of which we are not weary. I have received since the last information you had from me 5l. 17s. 4 1/4d., besides 1l. 10s. for the rent of the Orphan-Houses."

On Sept. 28th, while I was at Teignmouth, a brother asked me about the funds for the Orphans, being willing to help, and I had reason to believe considerably, if they were in need. Though I knew not for a certainty that there was one shilling in hand in Bristol, yet for the Lord's sake I declined telling him any thing about the funds, in order that the work might evidently be carried on by dealing with the Lord Himself.

On Sept. 28th we left Teignmouth for Plymouth, being taken by the love of a brother from Teignmouth to Newton Bushel in his own little carriage. At Plymouth we found again a kind brother waiting at the coach office, to receive us. He took us to his house and lodged us till our departure, on Oct. 6th. During my stay at Plymouth, I was stirred up afresh to early rising, a blessing, the results of which I have not lost since. That which led me to it was the example of the brother in whose house I was staying, and a remark which he made in speaking on the sacrifices in Leviticus, "That as not the refuse of the animals was to be offered up, so the best part of our time should be especially given to communion with the Lord." I had been, on the whole, rather an early riser during former years. But since the nerves of my head had been so weak, I thought, that, as the day was long enough for my strength, it would be best for me not to rise early, in order that thus the nerves of my head might have the longer quiet. On this account I rose only between six and seven, and sometimes after seven. For the same reason also I brought myself purposely into the habit of sleeping a quarter of an hour, or half an hour, after dinner: as I thought I found benefit from it, in quieting the nerves of my head. In this way, however, my soul had suffered more or less every day, and sometimes considerably, as now and then unavoidable work came upon me before I had had sufficient time for prayer and reading the Word. After I had heard the remark to which I have alluded,

I determined, that whatever my body might suffer, I would no longer let the most precious part of the day pass away while I was in bed. By the grace of God I was enabled to begin the very next day to rise earlier, and have continued to rise early since that time. I allow myself now about seven hours' sleep, which, though I am far from being strong, and have much to tire me mentally, I find is quite sufficient to refresh me. In addition to this I gave up the sleeping after dinner. The result has been that I have thus been able to procure long and precious seasons for prayer and meditation before breakfast; and, as to my body, and the state of the nervous system in particular, I have been much better since. Indeed I believe that the very worst thing I could have done for my weak nerves was, to have lain an hour or more longer in bed than I used to do before my illness; for it was the very way to keep them weak.-- As this may fall into the hands of some children of God who are not in the habit of rising early, I make a few more remarks on the subject.

I. It might be asked, how much time shall I allow myself for rest? The answer is, that no rule of universal application can be given, as all persons do not require the same measure of sleep, and also the same persons, at different times, according to the strength or weakness of their body, may require more or less. Females also, being generally weaker in body, require more sleep than males. Yet, from what I can learn, it is the opinion of medical persons, that men in health do not require more than between six and seven hours sleep, and females no more than between seven and eight hours; so that it would be rather an exception, for a man to require more than seven and a woman more than eight hours. But my decided advice, at the same time, is, that children of God should be careful not to allow themselves too little sleep, as there are few men who can do with less than six hours sleep, and yet be well in body and mind, and few females who can do with less than seven hours. Certain it is that for a long time, as a young man before I went to the university, I went to bed regularly at ten and rose at four, studied hard, and was in good health; and certain also, that since I have allowed myself only about seven hours, from the time of my visit at Plymouth in Oct. 1839, I have been much better in body, and in my nerves in particular, than when I was eight or eight hours and a half in bed.

II. If it be asked, but why should I rise early? The reply is, to remain too long in bed is 1. waste of time, which is unbecoming a saint, who is bought by the precious blood of Jesus, with his time and all he has, to be used for the Lord. If we sleep more than is needful for the refreshment of the body, it is wasting the time with which the Lord has intrusted us as a talent, to be used for His glory, for our own benefit, and the benefit of the saints and the unbelievers around us. 2. To remain too long in bed injures the body. Just as when we take too much food, we are injured thereby, so as it regards sleep. Medical persons would readily allow, that, the lying longer in bed than is needful for the strengthening of the body, does weaken it. 3. It injures the soul. The lying too long in bed, not merely keeps us from giving the most precious part of the day to prayer and meditation, but this sloth leads also to many other evils.--Any one need but make the experiment of spending one, two, or three hours in prayer and meditation before breakfast, either in his room, or with his Bible in his hand in the fields, and he will soon find out the beneficial effect which early rising has upon the outward and inward man. I beseech all my brethren and sisters into whose hand this may fall, and who are not in the habit of rising early, to make the trial, and they will praise the Lord for having done so.

III. It may lastly be said, but how shall I set about rising early? My advice is, 1. Commence at once, delay it not. Tomorrow begin to rise. 2. But do not depend upon your own strength. This may be the reason why, before this, you may have begun to rise early, but have given it up. As surely as you depend upon your own strength in this matter, it will come to nothing. In every good work we depend upon the Lord, and in this thing we shall feel especially how weak we are. If any one rises that he may give the time which he takes from sleep, to prayer and meditation, let him be sure that Satan will try to put obstacles in the way. 3. Do trust in the Lord for help, You will honour Him, if you expect help from Him in this matter. Give yourself to prayer for help, expect help, and you will have it. 4. Use, however, in addition to this, the following means: a, Go early to bed. If you stay up late, you cannot rise early. Let no society and no pressure of engagements keep you from going habitually early to bed. If you fail in this, you neither can nor ought to get up early, as your body requires rest. Keep also particularly in mind, that neither for the body nor the soul is it the same thing, whether you go to bed late and rise late, or whether you go to bed early and rise early. Even medical persons will tell you how injurious it is to sit up late, and to spend the morning hours in bed; but how much more important still is it to retire early and to rise early, in order to make sure of time for prayer and meditation before the business of the day commences, and to devote to those exercises that part of our time, when the mind and the body are most fresh, in order thus to obtain spiritual strength for the conflict, the trials, and the work of the day. b, Let some one call you, if possible, at the time which you have determined before God that you will rise; or procure, what is still better, an alarum, by which you may regulate almost to a minute the time when you wish to rise. For about 12s. a little German clock, with an alarum, may be bought almost in every town. Though I have very many times been awakened by the Lord, in answer to prayer, almost to the minute when I desired to rise; yet I thought it well to procure an alarum, to assist me in my purpose of rising early: not indeed as if it could give the least help, without the Lord's blessing, for I should remain in bed, notwithstanding the noise of the alarum, were He not to give me grace to rise; but simply looking upon it as a means. c, Rise at once when you are awake. Remain not a minute longer in bed, else you are likely to fall asleep again. d, Be not discouraged by feeling drowsy and tired in consequence of your rising early. This will soon wear off. You will after a few days feel yourself stronger and fresher than when you used to lie an hour or two longer than you needed. e, Allow yourself always the same hours for sleep. Make no change, except sickness oblige you. .

Plymouth, Oct. 1. Today my soul was again especially drawn out in prayer for the dear Orphans. I not merely asked the Lord that He would still continue to supply their need, but I was so fully assured that He had sent the necessary means since I last heard, that I was enabled to praise Him for having done so. Immediately after I had praised Him, but while I was yet on my knees, came another letter from brother T., dated Bristol, Sept. 29, in which he writes thus:

"The Lord's help has been graciously continued to us since I wrote last. Ever since your absence, the supplies have come in so seasonably, that I have not had occasion, until now, of opening the boxes in the Orphan-Houses. There came in, since my last account, from a sister 2s. 6d., with Ecclesiastes ix. 10, 1l.. 1s. 6d., through Mr. C. of Bath, 2l. 3s. 4d., from the boxes 14s. 6 1/2d., from A. M. B. 5s. Some apples besides have been given, some old clothes, and a large bath to be sold or used. I gave on Thursday to the sisters 10l., and today for the Boys'-Orphan-House 1l. 10s. After this I have in hand 1l. 3s. 8 3/4d., to be multiplied as the Lord wills. I had written thus far, and was on the point of writing that we expected sister E. home this evening, when the door-bell rang, and sister E. came in, bringing a little packet of money, directed to you, from Hereford, enclosing a letter and ten sovereigns "for your labours of faith and love;" so that the remainder of the barrel of meal has been multiplied somewhat already. It is most seasonable help! It rejoices me that it has come in time, for you to have the intelligence with this letter. I have in hand 19s. for the other funds, therefore it seems well to me, if it should be needed before I hear from you, to take only 5l. for the Orphans; but, if it pleases the Lord to enable us to do without, I shall leave it untouched until you write. In addition to what I have written, I have just received 10s. and 1l. 9s. 3d. How gracious!"

The time from October 6th to the 17th I spent among the brethren at Bideford and Barnstaple, with great refreshment to my own soul, and was also allowed by the Lord to minister to them. The whole of my stay among the children of God in Devonshire has been very profitable to me. May my soul not lose the blessing of it! How the Lord uses our infirmity of body for the blessing of our souls! In my case also it was instrumental in communicating blessing to others. I was able to speak more frequently in public, while absent from Bristol, than I should have done under ordinary circumstances, had I remained in Bristol.

Barnstaple, Oct. 10. The day before yesterday I had 10s. given to me here for the Orphans; and yesterday 3l., which came in most seasonably, as will appear from the following letter which I received this evening from brother T.

Bristol, Oct. 8th, 1839.

"My dear Brother, we have continued to enjoy the gracious help of the Lord since I last wrote to you. Nearly up to that time the supplies had come in so seasonably, that the previous disbursements had scarcely ever been expended, before I was again able to make a fresh one. Since then, however, we have been twice a little straitened. On Friday evening we were in prospect of Saturday's necessities, and had nothing to meet them, except the money about which I was in doubt from not having received directions from you. I had already used 5l. out of the 10l. which had been sent, and now, after waiting till it was actually needed, we thought it an indication, as none had been sent, that this should all go to the Orphan-Houses. On Monday again more money was needed than I had in hand, but we were in expectation of help. After dinner, as nothing had come in, I thought it well to open the boxes, thinking, that, although I had opened them so recently, I had no right to presume that the Lord had not had time to pour into them. The expectation was not in vain; for in the box at the Boys'-Orphan-House I found 1l. 0s. 1 1/2d., in the box at the Girls'-Orphan-House 7s. 1d. At the latter place I met sister A. who gave me 3s. for things that she had sold. Thus we were most graciously helped through Monday. Then, in the evening, at the meeting I received from sister B. 2s., and through sister C. 11s. I had opened the box at the Infant-Orphan-House on Monday, and found it empty. But today, finding the 13s. insufficient, and being told that something had been put in, I opened it, and found 3s. 6d., which nicely helped us through. And we are now looking to the Lord for more. In the mean time I shall this morning attend to the sale of whatever has been given to be sold. It comforts us to know you are praying for us," &c.

The money which I had received yesterday and the day before yesterday here, at Barnstaple, and two weeks ago at Teignmouth, enabled me now to send off at once 5l.

On Oct. 17th I returned to Bristol, with renewed strength, for active service.

Oct. 17. Bristol. The Lord has been again very gracious as it regards the funds; for during the last three days, while I was at Barnstaple, I received from a sister 5s., two rings, and a brooch. From another sister a gold watch, to be sold for the Orphans. From a brother a seal, two ear-rings, and a brooch. From a third sister sixteen books to be sold; also 4l., the produce of a veil. From a fourth sister 2l. 10s., and from a fifth 1l., and from five others 8s. 9d. In addition to this I found when I came home, that though my fellow-labourers had been greatly tried a few days previous to my return, so much so, that, when the 5l. arrived which I sent from Barnstaple, they were in greater poverty than they ever had been; yet, within the last days, several pounds had come in, and yesterday, over and above all this, arrived 15l. from London for some articles which had been sent there to be sold. What can we render unto the Lord for all His benefits!

Oct. 19. The Lord is still pouring in bountifully! This morning 10l. was sent from Worcester, and a sister brought 7l., being the produce of the sale of ladies' baskets, which she and some other sisters are making for the benefit of the Orphans. This last case shows what various means the Lord uses to provide for our need; yet all comes without one single individual being asked to give help; for to the Lord alone we speak about our need. We are now again comparatively rich, i. e. we have means in hand to meet the current expenses of about eight days, which has been only two or three times the case during the last fifteen months.

Oct. 30. A little boy brought me a letter, given to him by a gentleman and lady in the street, as he said, to take to my house. The letter contained these words with a five pound note: "The enclosed 5l. accept for the benefit of the Orphans, in the name of the Lord Jesus."

Nov. 5. Today an Orphan was brought from Bath, and a lady sent by her servant, the aunt of the child, a sovereign for the Orphans, when there was but 3s. 11d. in hand. It has been thus repeatedly, that when orphans have been brought, and we had no money, or scarcely any, that the Lord sent a little with these poor children. It never is with us any question, whether there is much or little money in hand, so far as it regards the reception of children; but only, whether there is room.

Nov. 8. We are now again quite poor. The Lord gave us to know more than usually from Oct. 17th to Oct. 31st what it is to abound, and now we know again what it is to be poor. It would have been desirable to have had 3l. today, but only 1l. 3s. 11d, was in hand, which I sent off. In our need we were led to open the boxes in the Orphan-Houses, which had not been done for some weeks, and in them was found 16s. 2 1/2d. To this one of the labourers added 9s. By this 2l. 9s. 1 1/2d. we could meet those expenses which needed to be met, and we were thus helped through the day.

Nov. 9. Saturday. 3l. 0s. 6d. was required today, in order comfortably to meet the present demands, but not one penny was in hand. Between ten and eleven I went to the Girls'-Orphan-House, to meet with my fellow-labourers for prayer. Only 2s. had come in. This was all I could leave. There was every thing in the houses which was required for the moment, and I proposed that we should meet again for prayer in the afternoon at four. When we did so, one of the labourers gave 8s. 6d., another 10s., another 5s. 6d., so that I had as much to give to the matrons as would provide comfortably all the necessaries for the children till Monday morning; only the usual quantity of bread could not be taken in. About half an hour, after we had separated, came in 1l. 10s., the produce of the sale of a shawl, which a sister from Devonshire had given for that purpose some days since. Thus we had altogether 2l. 16s., whereas when the day commenced we had no natural prospect of any thing. This is a new sweet encouragement. Besides this, our Father has given us another proof of His continued care, in that twenty sacks of potatoes and a small barrel of herrings have been sent for the Orphans.

Nov. 11. Monday morning. Yesterday, when, as just related, there was not a penny in hand, there was given to me, with Ecclesiastes ix. 10, ten shillings. This morning came in 1l. 10s, more, Soon afterwards a note was sent to me from the Orphan-Houses, to say that the need of today would be 3l. JUST WHILE I WAS READING THE NOTE I received another, including a sovereign, which a sister from Devonshire had given to one of the brethren for the Orphans. Thus I had just the 3l. which was needed. A few minutes after came in 1s. more.

Nov. 12. The need of today was 2l. As only 1s. had been left in hand yesterday, and no more than 6s. had come in, we were again in a strait. But I was not looking at the little in hand, but at the fulness of God. I sent off the little which I had. In the afternoon we met for prayer. I then found that 2s. 6d. had been taken out of the box in the Infant-Orphan-House, and that 4s. more had come in by the sale of some old books. To this one of the labourers added 2s. 3d., all she had of her own. After prayer came in 2s. 6d., which had been given while we were in prayer. In the evening we met again for prayer, when another labourer gave 3s. 4d. Thus, in our deep poverty, we got together this day 1l. 0s. 7d., which supplied our absolute necessities. We were this afternoon so reduced, till the Lord sent a little help, that there were no means to provide breakfast for tomorrow, for the children in the Boys'-Orphan-House.

Nov. 13. Nothing has come in. Our need is even greater today than yesterday, on account of our not having been able yesterday to take in the usual quantity of provisions. In this our need I packed up the books, which had been intended for sale on Aug. 22, when the Lord sent such a rich, supply, before they were actually disposed of. To them one of the labourers added some of his own, and a few other articles. Also some old jackets, which had been sent, were packed up to be disposed of. At twelve I met with my fellow-labourers for prayer.

There was every thing in the houses which was needed for dinner, but there were no means to get milk for tea. (The children have milk and water at tea time.) Three of my helpers went out to dispose of the articles. At four in the afternoon I received the information that 14s. had come in, for some of the things which were disposed of. One of my fellow-labourers had besides disposed of an article of his own for 1l. 5s. This 1l. 19s. enabled us to take in bread as usual, and to defray the other necessary expenses. We had never been lower in means than yesterday and today. Yet my soul, thanks to the Lord! was also yesterday and today in perfect peace. My helpers seem also quite in peace. This evening I received 2s. 6d., and 11s. with Ecclesiastes ix. 10. This little money is as precious, as at other times 100l. would have been, because it is a fresh proof that our Father still cares for us. The money was given to me just after I had been speaking on these words: "But I am poor and needy; yet the Lord thinketh upon me." Whilst speaking I was able, in a measure, to realize the preciousness of the truth contained in those words, and after speaking my Father gave me a fresh proof that He is thinking upon me.

Nov. 14. I took the 13s. 6d. which was given last evening, early this morning, to the Orphan-Houses, where I found that 10s. 6d. had come in by the sale of a Hebrew Old and a Greek New Testament, which a brother had given who had more than one copy; and 1s. 6d. for another book. This 1l. 5s. 6d. has been divided, in the hope that our kind Father will remember us before the day is over, and send in more. This afternoon, when we met for prayer, I found that 18s. more had come in for some articles which had been sold. We have had thus 2l. 3s. 6d. this day to divide for housekeeping. By the good hand of the Lord upon us, there has been every thing really needful. May the Lord look upon us, and help us further! Surely, He will do it!

Nov. 15. We are still in deep poverty. Nothing had come in by four o'clock in the afternoon, when I went to meet with my fellow-labourers for prayer. I did not go in the morning, because I knew that there was every thing which was needed till the afternoon. When I came I found that a sister had given 2s. 6d.; a new Bible which one of the labourers had given, who had more than one old copy, had been sold for 10s.; also 2s. had come in, and 1s. 4d. for some other articles which had been sold. This 15s. 10d. supplied that which was absolutely needed for today. We are still of good courage. We are sure that the Lord, in His own time, will deliver us out of the trial; for were our poverty more than a trial of faith, had the Lord in anger shut up His hands, we should not receive any thing at all. But this is not the case. For even this very day two sacks of potatoes were sent by the same brother who sent twenty sacks a few days since, with the promise to send still more. We have no means to lay in a stock for the winter, else we should have bought, perhaps, fifty or sixty sacks; but our kind Father does it for us. There has been also a toy chest of drawers promised for sale.

Nov. 16. Our prayer was last evening, in particular, respecting the necessities of today, as two days' provisions would be needed, it being Saturday. Besides this, about 2l. 10s. was needed to pay the weekly salaries of the brethren and sisters who labour in the Day-Schools. For all these demands there was nothing in hand, nor have we any more needless articles to dispose of; and useful ones we do not consider it right to sell, as our Father knows our need. When we met about twelve o'clock this morning, I found that last evening there had been Bibles unexpectedly sold to the amount of 1l. 11s. 6d., and about 10s. had been given besides. Thus we had nearly enough for the School-Fund. Moreover, 15s. had come in for the Orphan-Fund. A large sea-chest was given by a brother several months since, for the benefit of the Orphans, which had never been disposed of, and which, in this our great need, was sold for 15s. Yet this 15s. was needed to pay what was due for washing; and, therefore, we had still nothing to take in provisions with. It occurred to one of the labourers, that there might be a little advanced on his watch, of the money which had been laid by for rent, as had once or twice before been done; and that the watch might be sold at quarter-day, in case there should not come in enough to make up the deficiency. Yet even this plan we did not any longer think to be quite Scriptural, as he needs the watch in the Lord's service, and as our Lord is so kind, that He would otherwise send us means, were it well for us. In short, it appeared to us quite clear, that while we ought, in such a strait, to dispose of things which we do not need, nothing ought to be disposed of which is needed, in order that the Lord's own deliverance might be so much the more manifest. All we could think of for sale was five pewter dishes, which had been given nearly four years ago, but which were never used, as they were not convenient. These we agreed should be sold. About four o'clock this afternoon I received 2l. 2s., which a brother and sister had brought from Leicestershire. With this I went joyfully to the Orphan-Houses. There I found that 9s. 6d. had come in for the pewter dishes; one of the labourers had given 10s. for the Orphans, and 10s. for the School-Fund. (There had come in 2s. more for the other funds. All demands were met, and there was 1s. 6d. over.) Besides this, one of the labourers had sold a book of his own for 4s., and another labourer gave two pairs of new gloves, and four gentlemen's stocks. One pair of the gloves had been sold. Thus altogether had come in 4l. 2s. 3d., and therefore about 1l. 10s. more than was needed. We are now brought to the close of one more week. This has been, perhaps, of all the weeks the most trying. So much prayer, and so little coming in, I never knew. Yet, by the grace of God, I was sure that help would come, after the trial of faith was over. During the whole of this week, greatly as we have been tried, and though twice no stock of bread could be taken in, yet there has been nourishing food at every meal, and neither the children nor any other person can have perceived our poverty. About 13l. has been spent even this week for housekeeping in the three Orphan-Houses.

Nov. 18. Monday. The Lord has kindly sent in since Saturday evening 3l. 18s. 3 1/4d., and thus our need for today is supplied. On Saturday evening the produce of an orphan-box, 5s. 1 1/4d., was given; and last evening a sister gave two sovereigns to brother Craik, waiting for him a long time in the chapel, till she could see him. She might have delayed giving it till another time, as she had to wait so long; but the Lord knew our need. There were also sent eight sack of potatoes, by the same brother who had sent twenty-two sacks before.

Nov. 19. As there was not enough money in hand for the necessities of today, we were again as poor as on Saturday. Between three and four in the afternoon the milk is generally taken in; but in the Boys'-Orphan-House there was not money enough to meet this small expense. However, the Lord knew our need, and sent us at two o'clock 13s., which helped us comfortably through the day. A sister had purposed in her heart to give 3d. a week for the Orphans, and she felt herself stirred up to bring the yearly amount now, in this our extremity.

Nov. 20. This has been a day of deep poverty. Nothing but the 13s., above referred to, came in yesterday, which was scarcely enough to meet yesterday's usual need. My mind, by the grace of God, was not at all cast down; but I felt it rather trying, that the abundance of my other engagements had not allowed me to meet with my fellow-labourers, either yesterday or today, for prayer. This evening I had a note from the Boys'-Orphan-House, to state that a lady had sent two dozen of boys' shirts, which she had made herself, with which she sent 5s. to get them washed. This 5s, enabled us to meet that which was absolutely needful. [I mention here, that while our usual current expenses are about 2l. 10s. daily for housekeeping in the three houses; yet we might, in case of need, do for one or two days with as little as yesterday and today, as there are generally potatoes and meat in the house, and a stock of bread for two days, in order that the children may eat stale bread.] Without this 5s. we should have been unable to procure all that was absolutely needed. This our kind Father knew, and therefore He sent it. There were also given two quarterns of bread by one of the bakers, which made up the usual quantity. Moreover five and a half sacks of potatoes were sent by the brother who sent the others, making in all 35 1/2 sacks.

Nov. 21. This morning one of the labourers gave 7s., in order that there might be means to take in milk. Between ten and eleven o'clock we met for prayer, and I found that 10s. had come in for a toy chest of drawers, which in this our great need had been sent for sale. Besides this 6d. had been taken out of the box in the Infant-Orphan-House. This 17s. 6d. enabled us to provide the dinner, and to take in a little bread in two houses, even as much as would be enough for breakfast tomorrow; but there was 4s. 6d. needed to buy bread for the Boys'-Orphan-House, as there was only enough for today. When we met again this afternoon, 3s. had come in, as one of the labourers had sold a few old books. Another labourer gave 1s. 6d., and thus we had also the 4s. 6d., which was needed for bread. After prayer, it was mentioned that a sister, a servant, who is out of a situation, had been this afternoon to see the Orphan-Houses, and had put something into the box at the Girls'-Orphan-House. The box was opened, and half-a-crown was found in it. This money was, in our deep poverty, as acceptable as 50l. at other times might have been. We rejoiced when we saw it, for it was a fresh proof to us, that, not in anger, but only for the trial of our faith, we are so poor. This 2s. 6d. provides us with the means to take in milk tomorrow morning, so that we shall have everything which is needed till after breakfast tomorrow, but then there is neither bread, nor meat, etc. remaining for dinner. Our comfort, however, is: "The morrow shall take thought for the things of itself. Sufficient unto the day is the evil thereof." Matt. vi. 34. We separated very happy in God, though very poor, and our faith much tried.

Nov. 22. Our poverty had now become very great. Greater it had never been. Yet, the Lord be praised! I was as comfortable as ever; for I was sure we were only for the trial of our faith in this state. Had the Lord shut up His hand iii anger, He would not have continued to give us, even during this week, from time to time, tokens of His care over us. I said this morning: "Man's necessity is God's opportunity" is a proverb of the world, and how much more may we, His children, now look to Him in our great need. I knew we must have help in some way, as now it had come to the greatest extremity, there being in none of the houses anything for dinner, except potatoes, of which we have an abundance. At ten this morning I was informed that a large box, bearing my address, had arrived at one of the Orphan-Houses. I set off immediately, and found it was from the neighbourhood of Wolverhampton. It contained 12l. for the Orphans, 1l. 11s. 10d. for the other Funds, 4 yards of flannel, 9 yards of calico, 12 yards of print, 4 1/2 yards of coloured cotton, 4 yards of stuff, 2 pairs of stockings, and 3 1/4 yards of brown holland. Besides this, there were in it the following articles for sale: 2 decanters and stands, 4 glass salt cellars, 3 scent bottles, a set of cruets and stand, 5 beer glasses, 7 chimney ornaments, 3 tortoise-shell combs, 3 fans, 2 silver vinaigrettes, 2 silver shoe-buckles, 2 waist buckles, 2 silver salt-cellars, 1 pair of knives and forks with silver handles, a small silver toasting fork, 9 silver coins, three gold rings, 4 pairs of ear-rings, 3 brooches, a cornelian heart, a silver seal, 1 pair of silver studs, 1 gold watch key, 1 silver pencil case, 5 pairs of bracelets, 5 necklaces and 1 urn rug. The joy which I and my fellowlabourers had when all these things lay before us, cannot be described; it must be experienced in order that it may be known. It was two hours and a half before the dinner time, when the help was granted. The Lord knew that the Orphans had no dinner, and, therefore, did He now send help.--This morning also a brother sent to the Girls' Orphan-House to ask whether the treacle-cask was empty, and if so, to send it by the messenger, that it might be filled.

Nov. 24. Today 5l. came in again with Ecclesiastes ix. 10, besides 1l. 10s. for the rents.

Nov. 27. Today again some money was needed for housekeeping. But as a little had come in yesterday and today, we had enough.

Nov. 28. Last evening 10s. came in, which was just enough to supply this day's need. We are now again penniless.

Nov. 29. A great part of the articles, which were sent this day week from the neighbourhood of Wolverhampton, have now been disposed of for 5l. 11s.; we are, therefore, supplied for today and tomorrow.

Dec. 2. Since the last money has been given out for housekeeping, only 1l. 12s. has come in but as 1l. 10s. of this had been given for the rents, I had only 2s. in hand, when brother B., the master at the Boys'-Orphan-House, came this morning, and told me that the need of today would be at least 2l. I gave him the 2s. which I had, and proposed that we should pray together for more means. WHILE WE WERE IN PRAYER, a brother called. After prayer brother B. left me, and the brother who had come gave me 5l. As soon as he had left, I went joyfully with the money to the Orphan-Houses, to prevent the bakers being sent away. This evening I received still further 2l. Thus the Lord has richly supplied our need for today and tomorrow.

Dec. 3. The Lord has remembered again our need for tomorrow. I received today from Liverpool 15s.; and from a brother in the neighbourhood of London, who had been staying here for a season, 5l.; also 1l. by the sale of some articles.

Dec. 4. It has been repeatedly our prayer during the last month and in the beginning of this, that the Lord would be pleased to give us again so much means, before the time of the public meetings, which are fixed for the 10th, 11th, and 12th, of this month, that, when we speak about His dealings with us during this year, we might also respecting the close of it have again to speak, to His praise, of the abundance which we had in hand. At the end of last year we made the same request, and the Lord granted it. Now today, as an answer to this our often repeated request, I received from the East Indies 100l., to be laid out for the Orphans, or the other objects of the Institution. Respecting this money it is to be noticed: 1. The great distance from whence it is sent. 2. That it comes just now, and thus enables us to speak at the meetings of this rich supply after our trials. 3. It furnishes us with means to order Bibles, as one half of the money will be taken for the other funds; there having been a great inquiry for Bibles lately, and we have not been able to meet the demand, for want of means. Respecting this point also we have prayed repeatedly, and now the Lord has answered our petition. How very precious it is to wait on the Lord! What an abundant proof have we in this donation, that all our late straits, as it regards means, were only allowed for the trial of our faith! This evening came in still further 1l. 5s.

Dec. 9. Since Dec. 4 several small donations have come in, so that unto the last day of this fourth year of the Orphan-work the Lord has continued His kindness to us.

On Dec. 10, 11, and 12 we had public meetings, at which the account of the Lord's dealings with us in reference to the Orphan-Houses and the other objects of the Scriptural Knowledge Institution was given. During the whole of the past year, as formerly, the labourers who are engaged in the work had kept their trials and their joys of faith to themselves; but now we considered the time to have come, when, for the benefit of the church at large, and to the glory of our Lord, we should make our boast in Him.--It is now (i. e. on Dec. 10, 1839) five years and nine months since the Scriptural Knowledge Institution has been in operation. In addition to what has been said about the Lord's dealings with us, more especially in regard to the funds, I make a few more remarks, with reference to His kindness to us, in other respects, during the last year. 1. During the last year also we have been enabled to continue to provide all the needful expenses connected with the six Day-Schools, three for boys and three for girls. The number of the children, who are at present in them, amounts to 286. The number of all the children that have had schooling in the Day Schools, through the medium of the Institution, since its formation, amounts to 1795. 2. There are at present 226 children in the Sunday School. 3. There are 14 taught to read in the Adult School, and there have been about 130 adults instructed in that School, since the formation of the Institution. 4. There have been circulated during the last year 514 copies of the Scriptures, and 5592 since March 5, 1834. 5. There has been laid out during the last year 91l. 6s. for Missionary purposes. 6. There have been received into the three Orphan-Houses from Dec. 9, 1838, to Dec. 9, 1839, 16 orphans. There are at present 96 orphans in the three houses. The number of all the orphans, who have been under our care from April 11, 1836, to Dec. 9, 1839, amounts to 126.

I notice further the following points in connexion with the Orphan-Houses.

1. Without any one having been asked for any thing by us, the sum of 3,067l. 8s. 9 1/4d. has been given to us, entirely as the result of prayer to God, from the commencement of the work up to Dec. 9, 1839. 2. Besides this, there have also been sent many articles of clothing, furniture, and provisions, for the use of the Orphans. 3. Without our solicitation, three medical gentlemen (one for each house), have up to this time, kindly given their attendance and medicines gratuitously. 4. The hand of God is most manifest in that we have had so little sickness, considering that so

many persons during this autumn have been suffering from fever, etc. Even in this particular I desire publicly to acknowledge the Lord's peculiar kindness to us. 5. Though most of the children have been brought up in a very different manner from what we could desire, yet the Lord has constrained them, on the whole, during this year also, to behave exceedingly well, so much so that it has continued to attract the attention of all observers. 6. That, however, which gives us the chief ground for thankfulness, so far as the children are concerned, is, that in eight of them we perceive decided proofs of a real change of heart and of faith in our Lord Jesus Christ, so that they have been received into church fellowship. We are not surprised that these children, who are from 9 years old and upwards, have been converted; for the conversion of the orphans under our care has been a frequent subject of prayer among us, and that of late more than ever; so that we fully expect, if the Lord shall continue to give prayer for them, that soon many more will be brought to believe in the Lord Jesus.

The total of the expenses, connected with the objects of the Institution, exclusive of the Orphan-Houses, from Nov. 19, 1838, to Nov. 19, 1839, is 542l. 13s. The balance in hand on Nov. 19, 1839, was 18s. 5d. The total of the expenses connected with the three Orphan-Houses, from Dec. 9, 1838, to Dec. 9, 1839, is 960l. 9s. 2 3/4d. The balance in hand on Dec 9, 1839, was 46l. 8s. 1d.

Dec. 24. This morning we wanted again more money for the Orphans than there was in hand. It is only eight days since the last public meeting, when there was a balance of 46l. 8s. 1d. in hand. On this account we disposed of some silver articles and books which had been sent within the last days for the benefit of the Orphans, by which means we have enough for today and tomorrow.

Dec. 31. My health is much better than for years. My mental powers also are as good as they have been at any time during the last three years. I ascribe this to God's blessing, through the instrumentality of early rising, and plunging my head into cold water when I rise.

REVIEW OF THE YEAR 1839.

I. As to the church--68 brethren and sisters brother Craik and I found in fellowship when we came to Bristol.

573 have been admitted to fellowship since we came to Bristol.

641 would be, therefore, the total number of those in fellowship with us, had there been no changes. But

40 have fallen asleep;

33 are under church discipline

55 saints have left Bristol;

38 have left us, but are still in Bristol;

166 are therefore to be deducted from 641, so that there are only 475 at present in fellowship with us.

During the last year have been added 115, of whom 34 have been brought to the knowledge of the Lord among us.

II. As to my temporal supplies.

The Lord has been pleased to give me during the past year

1. By the Freewill Offerings through the boxes L137 4s. 5d.

2. By Presents in money, from saints residing in and out of Bristol L121 18s. 0d.

3. By Money through family connexion L42 0s. 0d.

4. By Presents in clothes, provisions, &c., which were worth to us at least L12 0s. 0d.

Altogether L313 2s. 5d.

January 1, 1840. Our usual meeting last night was most precious! We continued together from seven till half-past twelve. Of all the similar meetings which we have had, it was, according to my judgment, by far the best. Not more than five prayed; but there was much more real prayer than at former meetings.--This morning, about one hour after midnight, when our prayer meeting was over, I received a paper with some money sealed up in it for the Orphans. A few minutes afterwards I remembered that the individual who gave it was in debt, and I was aware she had been repeatedly asked by her creditors for payment; I resolved therefore, with out opening the paper, to return it, as no one has a right to give whilst in debt. This was done when I knew that there was not enough in hand to meet the expences of the day. About eight this morning a brother brought 5l., which he had received just then from his mother, for the Orphans. Observe, the brother is led to bring it at once! The Lord knew our need, and therefore this brother could not delay bringing the money. A few hours after I received 5l. more, and 8s. 5d., also 2s. 6d., so that we are now again supplied for three or four days.

Jan. 5. Besides the 10l. 10s. 11d, which came in on New-year's day, there came in on the 2nd and 4th 3l. 0s. 7d. But when now we were again without a penny, there came in 5s., and 6d., and 1s. Also 2l. with Ecclesiastes ix. 10, and 1l. 10s. for rent.

Jan. 7. Today, when there were again only a few shillings in hand, as since the 5th had come in only 3s., I gave myself to prayer, when, just after I had risen from my knees, a sister came and brought 1l., as a thank-offering to the Lord for the many mercies of the past year. There came in still further today, by ten different donations and the sale of two Reports, 2l. 17s.

Jan. 8. There were only a few shillings more in hand than was needed for housekeeping today. Nevertheless our kind Father remembered us before the day was over. A sister, a servant, gave me 15s.; also with Ecclesiastes ix. 10, came in 5l. 5s., from two sisters 6s, 1d., and by sale of Reports 3s.

Jan. 22. I have repeatedly asked the Lord for means to be able to order more Bibles, as two sorts were again exhausted. There is moreover scarcely enough money in hand to pay the teachers next Saturday. This afternoon I received from a sister 14l. 2s. 7d., which she had had in the Savings' Bank. She considered that this money would be better used in the Lord's work, than left in the Savings' Bank. Thus I was enabled to order some Bibles.

From Jan. 8th to 22nd came in 34l. 9s. 5d. for the Orphans, and the donations were so seasonable, that always either something was given, or articles which had been given for sale could be disposed of, before the last money had been expended. But as there was today again only very little in hand, I was led to open the orphan-box in my house, in which I found two papers, the one containing 10s., the other a 5l. note. In both papers was written Eccles. ix. 10. There came in today still further above 5l. Thus our Lord has sent us what we are likely to need for three or four days to come.

Jan. 25. I have been much in prayer this week about going to Germany: 1, To see certain brethren who purpose to go as Missionaries to the East Indies; and 2, To see my father once more. I am led to go just now, instead of delaying it, because my health is again so failing, that it seems desirable I should leave Bristol at all events, and thus I could continue to serve in the work of the Lord, and yet attend to the benefit of my health at the same time. Lord, keep me from making a mistake in this matter!

Jan, 31, Since Jan. 22 several small donations came in for the Orphans, and several pounds by the sale of silver articles, trinkets, &c. But as I have had to pay out today 11l. 13s., we are now again very poor. For many days past we have been so helped, that money has always come in, before all was spent. Now there is only 1s. 5d. in hand. The Lord will provide! I feel quite comfortable, though in three days I shall have to leave the work for several week.--About three hours after I had written the above, came in 1l. 14s. 1 1/2d. In the afternoon I received still further from Tottenham for the Orphans 10l., and in the evening from Hereford 30l., of which latter sum there was 6l. for the Orphans, and 24l. for the other objects of the Scriptural Knowledge Institution. Thus the Lord will kindly allow me to leave a little money behind on my departure, and I have also a still further answer to my prayer for means to purchase Bibles, for which I have asked the Lord repeatedly, and which he began to answer by the donation which I received on the 22nd. I have received 5l. besides for the other objects.

Feb. 1. I have now felt quite sure for several days past, that I should leave Bristol for a season, and go to Germany. If the Lord permit, I shall leave the day after tomorrow.

Feb. 2. Today and yesterday has come in still further, before my departure, nearly 9l. for the Orphans. How kind of the Lord to send this money just now, on the eve of my leaving home!

Feb. 3. Today I left Bristol for Berlin.

On Feb. 5th I left London in the steamer for Hamburg. Though it had been so very stormy for several weeks past, the Lord gate us a very favourable passage; the first, as the captain said, which they had had for several weeks. We landed at Hamburg on the 7th at five in the afternoon. The porter who carried my things led me, as I afterwards found out, some by-way, either to save a long distance, or to get me into the city with my luggage, though it was after the custom-house hours. I did not understand this at first; but, when we were about to enter the city, he told me that that was not the proper way, but that if I would give to the custom-house officer, whom I should presently see at the entrance into the city, a small fee, he would let me pass. My reply was that I did not wish to do what was unlawful, nor should I give a fee to encourage what was unlawful, and that I would rather go a long way round, than get by such means into the city. Presently we arrived at the place at which the custom-house officer stood, who, on my telling him plainly that I had not the least wish to pass that way, if it were unlawful, saw that I was only a passenger, and that I had no wish to get into the city with goods which are not duty free, and therefore let me pass. This little circumstance proves afresh in how many little things the children of God may act differently from the world, to the glory of their Father, and how in going the Lord's way, we find it to be, even as far as this life is concerned, the easiest path.--About half an hour after, when I arrived at the hotel, a little circumstance served afresh to remind me, that the Christian, like the bee, might suck honey out of every flower. I saw upon a snuffer-stand in bas-relief, "A heart, a cross under it, and roses under both." The meaning was obviously this, that the heart which bears the cross for a time meets with roses afterwards. I applied it to myself, and this little event greatly cheered my heart in this place, where I was without the fellowship of a single believer.

I left Hamburg in the evening of Feb. 8th, travelled all night, all day, and the whole of the second night, and reached Berlin on the morning of the 10th. I confessed not the Lord Jesus on this long journey, which I record here to my shame; nor did I give any other testimony for Jesus in the steamer, than merely refraining from the light and trifling conversation of the party, and all this after I had had on my way from Bristol to London a fresh encouragement in conversing with a gay traveller addicted to drinking, who evidently listened with a measure of attention, and with a desire of having his chains broken.

From Feb. 10th to 20th I was in Berlin. I think it is likely that eight or nine brethren and sisters will go from hence to the East Indies.--After having been greatly helped by the Lord in my work, the first and special object of my journey to the Continent; mercifully kept by Him in the narrow path and in great peace, whilst surrounded with temptations on every side; and after having also seen afresh abundant reason to praise the Lord for all the way in which He had led me since I lived here in 1828 and 1829; I left Berlin on the evening of Feb. 20th for Magdeburg, which I reached on the morning of the 21st, and on the same evening I arrived at my father's house.--In all human probability I now see my dear father the last time. He is evidently much weaker than he was two years ago, and coughs much more. What has the Lord done for me since I lived in the house where I am now! The two rooms where I am now most in prayer, reading the Word, and confessing His name, were those very rooms in which I sinned most, whilst living here many years ago. I have had again opportunity, most fully to bring out the truth about the work of the Lord Jesus before my father, whilst conversing a long time with a woman in his hearing, to whom I showed from the Scriptures, that we are to be saved, not by our own works, but simply by faith in the Lord Jesus, who bore the punishment instead of us, and who fulfilled the law in our room.

Feb. 24 and 25. I am still at Heimersleben. My dear father is very weak.

Feb. 26. This morning I left Heimersleben. I took leave of my father most probably for the last time. It has been a great pleasure to me, and I consider it a great privilege, to have been permitted by the Lord once more to see my father, once more personally to show him filial love and regard, and once more to set the truth before him. He has been again during the whole of this my stay most affectionate to me, as he was during my two former visits to him since I left the Continent to reside in England. How cheerfully should I have left him this morning, did I know him to be safe in Jesus! But, alas! he as yet is not resting upon Christ, though he is so far religious as to read prayers and the Bible.--After I had left him I went to my faithful and beloved friend, brother Stahlschmidt, at Sandersleben, but found him absent from home.

Brother Kroll, the servant of brother Stahlschmidt, [whom I have mentioned in the first part of my Narrative,] received me with much affection. When this brother first came to Sandersleben in 1829, there was scarcely a single true Christian besides his master in the little town. Soon afterwards he began to hold meetings, which were attended by the two or three who loved the Lord Jesus. These meetings were for a long time suffered to go on quietly; but when the Lord blessed them, and others were stirred up to care about their souls, brother Kroll had to appear before the magistrates, and was forbidden to hold them. When this was of no effect, (as he considered that he ought only to obey earthly rulers in things in which he could do so with a good conscience,) and they continued still to meet together, the police came into one of their meetings, and forced them to discontinue it. When even this availed nothing, the brethren were finally threatened that every one who attended these meetings should pay three thalers, and every one who read or spoke at them should pay five, which is a large sum in Germany for poor people. But notwithstanding all these obstacles, the few poor saints continue their meetings, but in secret, to be unmolested by the police. They have now neither a stated place nor a fixed time for their meetings. On the second and third evenings, whilst I was at Sandersleben, I met with them. On the second evening we were in the room of a poor weaver. The dear brethren would have me sit on the only chair which was in the room. It was a very small room, perhaps twice as large as the loom, which was in it. There were about twenty-five or thirty persons present, many of whom had seated themselves in and under the loom, and the rest sat on two or three little forms. These meetings were very precious. The very fact of going to them with the feeling of having to pay the fine, or to suffer an adequate imprisonment, should one be found there, makes them to be doubly valued; and I believe that the Lord's double blessing rests upon them. I spoke long both times; indeed, as long as I had strength, and the dear people seemed to eat the Word.--I have so circumstantially related these facts, that thereby the children of God in Great Britain may be led more highly to value their religious privileges, and to make good use of them whilst they are continued.

It is worthy of remark, that while the meeting at Sandersleben were permitted to continue, there was no believing clergyman in the little town; but about the time that they were forbidden, the Lord sent a brother who truly preaches the gospel. I had for some hours refreshing and most affectionate brotherly intercourse with Him. May the Lord let His blessing rest upon him, and help him to be a faithful witness for God in that dark neighbourhood!

I had travelled so fast, and stayed so short a time in the places where I had been, that I was obliged to leave Heimersleben without having received the letter which I had expected from my wife there, a matter of no small trial (as those who have been for some time at a great distance from home, know it to be); especially in my case, as, on account of the Orphans and the other work, besides my family, it was of so much importance for me to hear from time to time. I had arranged with my father to have the letter sent to me to Sandersleben, by an express messenger, who could be obtained for a small remuneration. However, hour after hour passed away, on the 27th, and the messenger did not arrive. At last the time was gone by, as it was getting dark, and the person ought to have come at noon. I now lifted up my heart to the Lord, beseeching Him to give me grace to give up my own will in this thing. No sooner had I been brought into such a state, as to be TRULY content and satisfied with the will of the Lord in this matter, than the expected letter was handed over to me. The woman who brought it had lost her way in the morning, on account of a dense fog, which made her so late. I have frequently found, under similar circumstances, that after I had been brought into such a state as to be willing to give up my own will, whereby I was fitted to bear the blessing, the Lord gave me the desire of my heart, according to the truth of that word: "Delight thyself also in the Lord, and He shall give thee the desires of thine heart." Psalm xxxvii. 4.

Feb. 29. This morning I left Sandersleben. Towards the evening I reached Halberstadt, the town where I was from Easter 1816 to June 1821, at the Cathedral Classical School. I went to a certain small inn, known to me from the time that I lived at Halberstadt, both for the sake of quietness and to save expense, as I knew it to be more like a private boarding-house than an inn. After having had my supper, the innkeeper, who seemed to me a quiet and unassuming person, came into the room where I was, and began conversation with me. After a few moments I recognised in him a former schoolfellow of mine. The Lord now enabled me to tell him of my gay life, my conversion, my subsequent going to England, and of some of the Lord's dealings with me there. He listened with great attention, and was evidently affected by what I said. May the Lord bless to him my testimony for Jesus! I was thus afresh reminded of what grace has done for me. How kind of the Lord to direct me to that place!

March 1. This morning I saw an old friend of mine, a missionary to the Jews at Halberstadt. When first he went there he held meetings, which the few Christians of the town attended; but of late he has been obliged by the police to give them up. In that town of about 15,000 inhabitants, with, I think, seven large Protestant churches, there is not one converted clergyman, as this brother told me; and the few Christians that are there are not permitted to assemble themselves together. Brethren, you who live in Great Britain, be thankful for your religious liberty, and make use of it while the days of outward peace last!--About twelve this morning I left by the mail for Brunswick. The Lord enabled me to preach Christ to a young man, a painter, who, for the sake of improvement in his art, had travelled far and wide, and was now returning home from Vienna to his parents. He listened very attentively, in which I had a fresh proof that one never ought to look at natural appearances in proclaiming the truth; for I judged, before I began to speak to him, from his gay appearance, that he would quite laugh at what I might tell him about Jesus.--I saw again this afternoon, at Wolfenbuttel the inn from whence I ran away, when in debt, in the year 1821, and praised the Lord for His goodness to me since that time. Now, this evening, I am at Brunswick, and shall have again, through the Lord's kindness, rest during the night, as the mail does not leave for Hamburg until nine tomorrow morning.

March 8. London. I left Brunswick on the 2nd, and arrived at Hamburg in 24 hours. As there was ice in the Elbe, the London steamer could not get up to Hamburg, and I had therefore to go alone, in a hired carriage to Cuxhaven, about eighty miles, the most expensive journey that ever I made in my life, for it cost above 3l. 10s. Thus I had to travel three days and two nights, with the interruption of only five hours at Hamburg. I reached Cuxhaven at half-past eight in the evening on March 4th.--The fact of having thus to travel from Hamburg to Cuxhaven, that being the only way in which I could have got there in my circumstances, without losing the steamer, showed me afresh how one is step by step cast upon the Lord. A month since the Elbe was cleared of ice, and now, contrary to the expectation of all, the cold had returned to such a degree, that it was a second time innavigable.

March 3. I embarked this morning for London. I had conversation with two Russian Jews, who listened with great interest to all I said to them; but I did not tell them plainly that I believed Jesus of Nazareth to be the Messiah, as I fully purposed to do at the next conversation. After I had left them, they conversed with each other, and I could see from their countenances, that they either took me for a baptized Jew, or for a missionary to the Jews, on account of the peculiar way in which I had conversed with them. Presently one of them came and asked me what I thought of that Jesus. No sooner had I owned Him as the true Messiah and as my Lord and my God, than he began to blaspheme; and from that time, as long as we were on board, they shunned me; and I also felt that all I had to do was to show kindness to them by actions, but no more to converse with them about the Messiah, in order to keep them from blaspheming that holy name which is dear to my heart. My conversation with them had, however, an unexpected effect in another way. At the dinner table I was asked by one of the passengers about those Jews, who they were, etc., as my long conversation with them on the deck had been noticed. This led me, (in order that the conversation might be turned to profitable subjects, and that I might discover whether there was a Christian at the table), to throw out the remark, "how remarkable it is that the Jews, in all parts of the world, can be recognised as such; and are not mixed with other nations," etc. Immediately the captain replied, "this can only be explained by the Scriptures, and shows the Bible to be true," or something to that effect. I now, in agreeing with the captain, followed up the subject, and both after dinner and repeatedly during the passage had long and most interesting conversations with the captain, whom I found to be a true brother in the Lord, and from whom I separated most affectionately on our arrival in London.

On March 7th I landed in London, where I found two letters from my dear wife, from which I saw that up to the last the Lord had been dealing with her, as well as with me, in the greatest kindness, and had given also an abundance for the Orphans during the whole time of my absence.

March 9. I left London this morning, arrived this evening in peace in Bristol, and found my dearest Mary and all in peace. Truly, the Lord has abundantly blessed me and them while I have been from home!

During the whole time of my absence the Lord not only supplied all the need of the Orphans, but on my return I found more in hand than there was when I left. The donations, which came in during my absence, amount to between 80l. and 90l.

March 11. Today I received 19l. 19s., being a legacy left to me by a brother who fell asleep the beginning of last December. How richly does the Lord supply all my own temporal necessities!

March 22. Today, when there was not a penny in hand for the Orphans, I received the following donations: 3l. as the produce of the sale of ladies' baskets, an old crown piece, an old half-crown piece, and a Spanish dollar. Also 1s. With Eccles. ix. 10, was given 2l. 10s.

March 23. Today came in still further 1l. 2s. 6d.

March 25. All money was now again given out, when today came in by the sale of Reports 8s. 9d., and in small donations 1l. 5s. 11d.

March 26. On the 17th of this month 1 received the following letter, from a brother who several times had been used by the Lord as an instrument in supplying our need, and who also two months since sent 30l.

"I have received a little money from ----. Have you any present need for the Institution under your care? I know you do not ask, except indeed of Him whose work you are doing; but to answer when asked seems another thing, and a right thing. I have a reason for desiring to know the present state of your means towards the objects you are labouring to serve: viz, should you not have need, other departments of the Lord's work or other people of the Lord may have need. Kindly then inform me, and to what amount, i. e. what amount you at this present time need, or can profitably lay out."

At the time when this letter came, we were indeed in need, or at least it was desirable, as far as I had light, to have means, as I was just on the point of establishing an Infant-School, and as again some sorts of Bibles were needed in order to go on with the circulation of the Scriptures. Also in the Orphan-Fund there was only 2s. 3 1/2d. Nevertheless I considered that, as I have hitherto acted, (i. e. telling the Lord alone about our need), I ought to continue to do, as otherwise the principal object of the work, to be a help to the saints generally, by seeking to lead them to increased dependence upon God alone, through this Institution, would be frustrated. I answered therefore the letter, in substance, as follows:

"Whilst I thank you for your love, and whilst I agree with you, that, in general, there is a difference between asking for money, and answering when asked, nevertheless in our case I feel not at liberty to speak about the state of our funds, as the primary object of the work in my hands is, to lead those who are weak in faith to see that there is reality in dealing with God alone."

After having sent off the answer, I was again and again led to pray to the Lord in this way: "Lord, thou knowest that for Thy sake I did not tell this brother about our need. Now, Lord, show afresh that there is reality in speaking to Thee only about our need, and speak therefore to this brother, so that he may help us."

Today, in answer to this my request, this brother sent 100l., of which sum I shall take 20l. for the Orphans, and 20l.. for each of the other objects. Thus I have means for establishing the Infant-School, and for ordering more Bibles. Also the Orphans are again supplied for a week; for when the money came in there was not one penny in hand for them.

April 7. This evening I received information from my little half brother that my dear father died on March 30th. He was taken worse a few days after I left him. How kind of the Lord to have allowed me once more to see him! Had I gone to Germany at the time I first intended, he would most likely not have been alive to see me.--As I know not of one believer in the whole town where he lived, I cannot for a certainty ascertain any thing about his state before his death; but that which I do know gives me no proof of his having died in the faith of Christ. As to myself, I am sure of this, that it becomes me to adore that wonderful grace which plucked me as a brand out of the burning, and to say in reference to my dear departed father: "Shall not the judge of all the earth do right?" and in submission to the will of God to be satisfied with His dealings. This, through grace, I am able to do. Every true believer who has unconverted parents, for whose spiritual welfare he is concerned, can understand what joy it would have been to me to have heard a satisfactory account of a true change of heart in my dear father before his end; but as it has been otherwise, I know nevertheless that God will be eternally glorified even in this dispensation. During no period did I pray more frequently or more earnestly for the conversion of my dear aged parent, than during the last year of his life; but, at all events, it did not please the Lord to let me see the answer to my prayers.

April 9. Through the 20l. which came in on March 26, and a number of smaller and larger donations since then, we have had for the last twelve days more than usual. But now today our means were again reduced to 7s. 10d., when the Lord sent in 5l. through a brother in Bristol, who during this year also, as at former times, has been the instrument in the hands of God of repeatedly supplying our need when we were very poor.

We are on the point of sending some money to the East Indies for Missionary objects. Whilst I was on my knees respecting this object, 5l. was brought for it.

April 10. Today came in still further for the Orphans, with Eccles. ix. 10, 5l.; also 2l.

April 19. For several months past it had appeared to brother Craik and me, and to several other brethren who help us in the work of caring for the saints, that a part of the church meeting together at Gideon Chapel was a hinderance to our giving that clear and distinct testimony respecting the principles on which we meet, which we desire to give to the world and to the church at large in this city. As the Lord, however, had so abundantly blessed our labours in that place, in the conversion of sinners, and also in the building up of many saints, we felt that we ought to act in this matter with the greatest prayerfulness and consideration; and we had therefore many meetings for prayer and deliberation with several brethren. On this account it was likewise, that though we came as early as the 17th of January to the conclusion that it would be better to relinquish Gideon as a meeting place, we still deferred the matter for two months and a half longer, before we even mentioned our difficulties publicly. At last, on March 30th, we assembled with all the saints, and brother Craik and I stated to them our difficulties. The following is the substance of what was stated at the meeting.

Brief statement of certain difficulties connected with our continuing to retain the occupancy of Gideon Chapel, Newfoundland Street, Bristol.

In order to enter into the force of the following particulars, it is necessary to keep in mind the position which, as a body of saints, we seem called upon to maintain, in this city, before the church and the world. We meet simply as believers in Christ, without reference to any sectarian distinction, maintaining the Scriptures as our only rule of doctrine and discipline, and affording freedom for the exercise of any spiritual gift which the Lord may be pleased to bestow. We thus hold out a gathering place for all who believe in the Lord Jesus, and desire to confess His name, by obedience to His authority. Whatever impedes us, in this our great work, can only be suffered to continue, if the Lord Himself lays it upon us as a burden or chastisement. Nothing but necessity can justify our putting any obstacles in the way of the saints in this city, who, feeling the obligation of separating from every sectarian bond of union, would desire to meet with us.

I.

1. There seems no sufficient reason for holding our Lord's day morning meetings, for the breaking of bread, in two different places. See 1 Cor. xi. 20. The number is not too large to assemble in one place, and the extent of locality is not so great as to prevent it, except in the ease of invalids or of very aged persons: and the disadvantages of two meeting places are very serious. In this way of meeting the gifts are needlessly divided, as the gifted brethren are in two places instead of one; discipline is rendered very difficult to be executed, as it can scarcely be ascertained

who absent themselves, etc.; and impediments are thrown in the way of mutual intercourse and acquaintance, as the saints sometimes go to the one place, and sometimes to the other.

2. There are only four ways in which we can so arrange as to assemble every Lord's day morning, as a church, together. a, Bethesda may be given up, and the meeting of the saints maybe at Gideon. b, The meetings maybe alternately at each place. c, The meetings may be held at a third place intermediate, in respect of locality, between the two. d, Gideon may be given up, and Bethesda alone become the place of meeting for breaking of bread.

--In regard to the first two of these four arrangements, the size of Gideon puts a complete obstacle in the way, as there would not be sufficient room, were the saints and others, who would still attend, to meet together in that place. The third plan appears to be freest from all objections, could it be accomplished; but there is no one other place to be obtained sufficiently large for our purpose, and therefore, if it be granted that the profit of the saints and the glory of Christ seem to require our having one gathering place, till the number of the saints and the extent of locality on which they reside shall force us to have more than one: the only way in which, for the present, this can be accomplished is by our relinquishing Gideon, and having Bethesda as our only place of meeting.6

II.

But the above are not the only reasons why we should no longer continue to retain Gideon as a meeting place for the church.--We have reason to believe that several of our dear brethren, who have been in the habit of assembling there for worship, do not see with us in reference to the great leading principles on which we professedly meet. Ever since the removal of any restraint upon the exercise of whatever gift the Spirit may bestow, in connexion with the practice of weekly communion at Gideon, there has been dissatisfaction on the part of some. A few have left and gone to other places, some have been in the habit of remaining only as long as there is teaching or exhortation, and then leaving without breaking bread. We have reason to believe that several do not, in heart, acknowledge us as taught of God in regard to the changes, which we have introduced; or, if they feel unwilling to say so, yet they are inclined to retain their old way. Now, spiritual rule can only be continued over those who yield willing subjection: an unwilling submission on the part of those who are in the place "of the ruled," we deem no true subjection at all. Therefore, those who do not believe that matters are conducted amongst us in a Scriptural way, cannot comfortably continue in fellowship with us: and by yielding up to them the use of the Chapel, we take away all just cause of complaint.--On account of these reasons there would be no need of leaving a meeting place under other circumstances; but as, when brother Craik and I came to Gideon Chapel, we found saints there assembled together in fellowship who had contributed towards the purchasing and fitting up of the Chapel, and who had been in the habit of meeting together on different principles, it seems not Christlike either to force our light upon them, or to constrain them to leave us; but to give up the Chapel to them, as they do not, in heart, go along with us. It cannot be expected that, for the sake of pleasing even those whom we love in Christ, we should shrink back from carrying out any truth which the Lord may lead us into; and, therefore, if our brethren cannot heartily go along with us, it is better that nothing should be imposed upon them contrary to their convictions. If it should be said that for the sake of a few we thus separate from many: our reply is, that we separate from none of the saints; we only withdraw from a building, because it appears to us a hinderance to the manifesting of the truth, and, at the same time hold out a gathering place for all who feel that it would be for the edification of their souls, and the glory of God, that they should continue to meet with us. We invite all those who conscientiously can submit to the order which obtains amongst us, to continue in fellowship with us; and we purpose to provide a place of meeting to suit the convenience of the feeble and aged who would feel the distance of Bethesda to be an obstacle to their meeting habitually with the saints there.

III.

But in addition to those already mentioned, there is a third class of difficulties connected with retaining Gideon. The present character of the meeting for the breaking of bread there, is very far from fully exhibiting the principles on which we meet together. Unbelievers sitting among the saints, hinders our appearing to meet for the breaking of bread, and renders it necessary that a disturbing pause should intervene between the act of breaking bread and the other part of the meeting. We cannot have the breaking of bread at the commencement of the meeting, because of the confusion occasioned by the intermixture of those who are not in fellowship with us. To alter this, and to request all who are not in fellowship with us (except those belonging to the families of the saints) to sit by themselves, as is the case at Bethesda, would, we fear, produce increased dissatisfaction. Such a request moreover would not be Christlike, as long as from the construction of the building no comfortable sittings were reserved for any besides the saints themselves. Thus, by retaining Gideon, we are under the necessity of either marring our testimony to the church at large, or of deepening the dissatisfaction prevalent among several who are already in fellowship with us.--Again, the very construction of the place renders it unsuitable for a meeting of saints. Part of the sittings being pews, necessarily tends to give the appearance of a distinction between the very poor and the more respectable class. This distinction would need to be done away, and we have every reason to fear that some might feel personally aggrieved by the pews being taken away and replaced with benches. We have only of late understood that some of the pews are looked upon as private property. This is such a violation of the statement that the sittings are all free, that it could no longer be permitted. To require these unscriptural practices to be renounced, we have reason to apprehend, would be considered as an arbitrary act of rule, and might alienate the minds of those of our dear brethren who are still, in heart, attached to that to which they hare been accustomed in former years.

If it can be shown that the above difficulties are capable of being removed, or that any greater evil would attend the yielding up of Gideon than the evils which necessarily accompany our retaining it, then we are bound not to give it up. But, according to our present light, we see no way of reconciling the two objects, viz.: the retaining of Gideon, and the exhibiting a full, unhindered testimony to the truth of God. We repeat it, that we do not separate from any single individual in fellowship with us, we only leave the walls of a building, and invite those who feel called upon to separate from every sectarian system, and to meet where free exercise is afforded for every spiritual gift, to assemble with us at Bethesda.

In the case of those who are in ordinary health, the inconvenience attending the locality of Bethesda is a matter of very little consequence. Half an hour's earlier rising on the morning of the Lord's day, would be sufficient, in most cases, fully to meet the difficulty; and the consciousness, that the glory of Jesus and the true welfare of His church were thereby promoted, would far more than compensate for the amount of self-denial which the inconvenience arising from the distance would impose.--In reference to the weak, the sickly, and the very aged, who reside in the neigbourhood of Gideon, we trust, in the strength of the Lord, to make such ample provision for their comfort on the Lord's day, that they may have no reason to regret that Gideon has been relinquished. Lastly, as it regards the opportunities which will be lost, by giving up Gideon, of proclaiming the truth among believers, as well as preaching the gospel to the world, we intend, according to our ability and the measure of gift amongst us, to open places for those purposes in different parts of the city.

After we had fully stated our minds respecting our difficulties in continuing to meet, as a church, at Gideon Chapel, we were still quite willing to continue to occupy it as a preaching place, provided the brethren whose property the Chapel was (because of their having contributed towards the purchase and fitting up of the building,) were perfectly satisfied with our doing so. If this had been the case, all the difference would have been, that on Lord's day mornings Gideon Chapel would have been shut, and all the church would have met at Bethesda; but we should have been willing not only to preach in Gideon on the Lord's day evenings, and once or twice in the week, but also on the Lord's day afternoons instead of the morning meeting: so that even the unconverted, or the believers of that neighbourhood, who are not in communion with us, should have been no losers.--Whilst nothing was stated by any one, that showed us we had been mistaken in the conclusion to which we had come, a point was mentioned which soon brought the matter to a final decision. It was said that the giving up of one of the principal meetings on the Lord's day would be against the spirit of the trust deeds, as the Chapel was particularly intended to be a preaching place. Now, though we did not see it to be thus, as we meant to preach the Word, as before, at Gideon, if it could be done in perfect harmony with the owners of it; yet it seemed beyond a question that we could not retain the Chapel, whilst we appeared, even in the least to alienate the property from the use for which it was said to have been intended. We, therefore, were confirmed by this in our conclusion to give up the Chapel at once, and that entirely. [In order that the aged and infirm, and invalids who live in the neighbourhood of Gideon, might not be losers by the change, cars were provided, at the expense of the church, to convey them to the meeting for the breaking of bread at Bethesda; and a Chapel was rented in Callow-hill Street, near Gideon, in which, on the Lord's day and Thursday evenings the Word was ministered, It was very kind of the Lord to order it so that this chapel was at once to be had! Two years and a half afterwards, in October, 1842, we rented a still more suitable Chapel, in the heart of the City. On April 19th, 1840, we preached for the last time at Gideon, after having laboured there, with abundant blessing, for about eight years. Only three saints, as far as I know, out of about 250, who used to meet with us at Gideon, remained there. Nor has the Lord ceased to bless our labours since we left.]

April 27. Monday. The Lord knew that we were penniless, and should be in need of fresh supplies today for the Orphans, therefore He moved the hearts of some of His children to remember us, in answer to our prayer. Yesterday I received with Eccles. ix. 10, 5l., and 10s. from a sister who had lent this sum to some one, but never expected it again; and now, having unexpectedly received it, gave it to the Lord for the Orphans. 1l. 10s. was given for the rent of the Orphan-Houses. There was 2s. 6d. put anonymously into the box at Bethesda, and also 1l. This morning I was informed that 5l. had been sent to the Infant-Orphan-House. Thus the Lord has given for our need 13l. 2s. 6d.

Let us pause here a few moments, beloved reader! Let us adore the Lord's kindness! See how seasonably the Lord sends the help. As our need is, so He remembers us. It is not now and then that He is mindful of us, but continually. As surely as we stand in need of any thing, He sends it; be it money, provisions, clothes, or any thing else. We may be allowed to be poor, yea, very poor; we may have to pray again and again to our Father before the answer comes; we may be reduced so as to have from mal to meal to wait upon Him; yea, according to all outward appearance, the Lord may seem to have forgotten us:--but, amidst it all, as surely as we really need any thing, in His own time and way does He send help. Perhaps you may say; "But how would you do, in case there were a mealtime to come and you had no provisions for the children, or they really wanted clothes, and you had no money to procure them?" Our answer is, such a thing is impossible as long as the Lord shall give us grace to trust in Him, (for "whosoever believeth on Him shall not be ashamed,") and as long as He shall enable us to carry on the work in uprightness of heart. But should we be ever so left to ourselves as to forsake the Lord and trust in an arm of flesh, or should we regard iniquity in our heart i. e. wilfully and habitually do any thing, either in connexion with the work or otherwise, which is against the will of God, then we may pray and utter many words before Him, but He will not hear us, as it is written: "If I regard iniquity in my heart, the Lord will not hear me."

Psalm lxvi. 18. I, therefore, beseech all who love our Lord Jesus and who may read this, to entreat Him on behalf of all of us who are engaged in this work, that He would be pleased to continue to give us faith, and that He would keep us from living in sin.

May 2. Nothing having come in for five days, we were today again penniless. In answer to prayer 5s. 6d. came in, and some trinkets were sent, the names of which the donor does not wish to be known. Thus we were helped through this day.-- Observe here, how the Lord allowed five days to pass away without influencing the hearts of any to send us supplies; but the moment there is real need, the stream runs again.

May 3. Today the Lord sent in again some money for the Orphans. He knew we were penniless, and therefore answered our requests. Besides 1l. 10s. for rent, there came in 1l. 1s. from London, and 2l. from the Isle of Wight.

May 4. By what came in yesterday, we were supplied for today; but the Lord sent today still more, as that which came in yesterday was only enough for today. There was given in money 7l., of which 3l. was the profit of the sale of ladies' baskets, which are made by some sisters in the Lord for the benefit of the Orphans.

Last evening a brother was baptized, who on the first Lord's day of this year came with his intended wife to Bethesda Chapel. Both were in an unconverted state. They both were at the same meeting, through what brother Craik said, made to feel the power of the truth, and, in consequence, were led to Jesus and found peace in Him, and are now both in communion with us.--The Lord still condescends to use us as instruments. Today we conversed with seven persons about fellowship, and had to send away five, being worn out after we had seen the seven, one after the other. Only since April 1st, forty-one persons have come to us to speak about their souls. May the Lord in mercy give us helpers in the work, for truly the harvest is great; and may not our ingratitude for His abundant blessing upon our labours oblige Him to shut up His hands from continuing to use us!

May 6th. This evening I received 10l. for the Orphans, and 10l. for the Infant-School, which we are on the point of opening. Before our little stock is quite exhausted, (for there is yet 2l. left for the Orphans) the Lord has thus kindly sent a fresh supply. Thus also my prayer is answered in being able to give to two of the sisters in the Orphan-Houses some money for their personal expenses.

May 8. There are four believers staying at my house, and today we had only a few shillings of our own money left. I gave myself, therefore, to prayer for means for our own personal expenses. In answer to my request, I received this morning 5l.

May 10. Today five of the Orphans were received into fellowship and baptized. There are now fourteen of them in fellowship.

May 16. The need of today, as we were again penniless, led us to open the boxes in the Orphan-Houses, in which 2l. 0s. 2d. was found. There was given 5s. besides. In the evening came in still further a sovereign from a sister, a servant, with the following lines: The Lord has put it into my heart to send a sovereign to the Orphans. He indeed put it into my heart, which was once at enmity with God and would have said, lay it by, you may want it when you are old; but then I could not look towards heaven and say, I know my Heavenly Father will supply all my need; neither could I say, 'Abba, Father,' for I knew Him not."

May 17. Today the Lord has sent a little more, so that we have enough to meet the demands of tomorrow. There came in altogether 31. 9s. 6d.

May 22. Several small donations enabled us to supply the necessities of the last four days. When this day commenced, however, there was again not a penny in hand. But my eyes were directed to the Lord, and therefore my heart was at peace; I was fully assured that He would help this day also. About eleven I was informed that there was 19s. 3d. in hand, being the produce of the boys' knitting, and that also some old clothes, given for sale, had been sold for 3s. 6d., and one Report besides for 3d. To this one of the labourers added 4s. of his own, and gave a book besides for sale. Thus we had 1l. 7s., which was enough to meet the demands of this day.

May 26. By the sale of 166 little books which had been given to be disposed of, by a few shillings which came in for the children's needlework, by 4s. which had been taken out of the boxes in the Orphan-Houses, by a little money given by one of the labourers, by 10s. which came anonymously in a letter, and by the sale of some Reports--we were able to meet the demands since the 22nd. Today there was 1l. 2s. 8d. left in hand, but this was not quite enough for the need of the day. In the afternoon came in for needlework 11s. 6d., and there was 5s. left at the Infant-Orphan House. Thus we had enough, and a few shillings left for tomorrow.

May 26. Nothing had come in. My engagements kept me from going to the Orphan-Houses till seven in the evening, when the labourers met together for prayer. When we met I found that one of them had given 17s., which had been divided between the three houses. This, with the little which had been left yesterday, had procured all necessary articles. We are now very poor.

May 27. We met for prayer, at eleven this morning. No money had come in, but there was enough for dinner in all the houses. This morning the LAST COALS were used in the Infant-Orphan-House, and in the Boys'-Orphan-House there were ONLY ENOUGH FOR TODAY, and there was no money in hand to buy more. In this our need T.P.C. sent a load of coals. How kind of the Lord! A plain proof that not in displeasure, but only for the trial of our faith we are allowed to be so poor. We purpose to meet again at four this afternoon. May the Lord graciously be pleased to send help in the mean time!

Evening. The Lord has had mercy! A person bought some days since several articles, which had been given to be sold for the benefit of the Orphans, and owed 6l. 15s. This morning I asked the Lord to incline his heart to bring the money, or a part of it, as we were in such need. Just as I was going to meet for prayer with my fellow-labourers this afternoon, he came and brought 4l. But our kind Father showed us still further today, that only for the trial of our faith He had for a season withheld supplies; for there was given this evening with Eccles. ix. 10, 5l. There came in also 9s. for articles which had been put into the hand of a sister, who has taken on her the service of disposing of articles which are given for sale. Besides this, there were sent two boxes of new clothes, and some materials for clothes, from sisters in the Lord, residing in Dublin, which articles are worth several pounds. Thus the day, which had begun with prayer, ended in praise. But there is one thing more to be recorded respecting this day, as precious or more so than what has been said: I was today informed that the Lord has begun to stir up several of the boys to care about their souls.

May 28. The Lord has kindly sent in further supplies. A clergyman gave 2l.; and 5s. came in for Reports.

May 29. Today has come in still further 1l. 3s. 2d., and several trinkets which were sent from Barnstaple.

May 30. I took 1l. out of the box in my house.

May 31. When there was again not a penny in hand, the Lord sent in 2l. 2s.

June 6. This is Saturday. Several pounds were needed, as usual, for the Orphans; but there was not a penny in hand. In this our great need F. W., who often has been instrumental in supplying our need, and who lives many miles from Bristol, sent 5l. There came in 5s. besides. Thus we are helped to the close of one more week, in which our faith has been repeatedly tried. In the evening came in further, by sale of articles, 2l., and a donation of 10s.

June 7. Lord's day. Today came in 7l. 1s. 3d., to enable us to meet the necessities of tomorrow.

June 8. This evening eight German Missionary brethren and sisters, whom I have been for some time expecting, arrived in Bristol, on their way to the East Indies.

June 9. Again, when only 2s. 3d. was in hand for the Orphans, there came in from a considerable distance 2l.

June 10 and 11. These two days came in 1l. 0s. 4d., which was enough, with the little which had been left, to procure what was needed.

June 12. When there was nothing in hand, several articles of gentlemen's clothing, all worn, were sent for sale, which, being disposed of for 1l. 17s., we were helped through this day.

June 13. Today's need was met by a box of clothes coming from Worcester, which contained also 3l. 0s. 2d. There was also 11s. taken out of the box in my house.

June 15. 2l. 5s. 3d. came in yesterday and today, by which we were able to meet the necessary demands, and have 5s. left.

June 16. Some articles were sold for 11s., which had been given for sale. This, with the remaining 5s., met the necessities of the day.

June 17. Only 4s. has come in by children's needlework. This is all we have, to meet the need of today, except 2s. 6d., which I found in the box in my house, which our poverty led me to open. Evening. The Lord has had mercy upon us. A sister, to whom some time since some money was left, and whom the Lord has made willing to lay it all out in His service, having received a small part of what is coming to her, brought 5l. 10s. 6d. of it, this afternoon, for the Orphans. There came in still further this evening 2l.

For several days past I had been very poor in reference to my own temporal necessities, as well as in reference to the Orphans. Today we were especially poor, in both respects; but our kind Father remembered not merely the need of the dear Orphans, but gave me also some money for my own personal expenses. The same sister just referred to, who brought 5l. 10s. 6d. for the Orphans, brought me also 7l. for myself.

June 18. Today a new coat and waistcoat were given to me, for which I had repeatedly asked the Lord, as my clothes are now very old. As surely as I really need any thing, be it in money, or in any other way, my kind Father supplies the need.

June 19. The Lord has poured in still more abundantly today. A brother gave me 10l. for myself. Thus, after a season of more than usual poverty, the Lord sends a more than usual supply. How kind a Master do I serve!

June 21. Again, when there was not one penny in hand, came in today 6l. 10s. for the Orphans.

June 22. Tomorrow, the Lord willing, I purpose, with my wife, to accompany the three German brethren and the five German sisters to Liverpool who purpose to sail from thence. Under these circumstances it is desirable to leave at least a little money behind. This desire of my heart the Lord has granted; for this morning D. C. gave me 5l., and there came in by sale of articles 10s. 5d. In the evening a sister, who has left Bristol today, sent me by her mother 5l., having particularly requested her to let me have the money today, as she knew that I was going away tomorrow.

This evening we had an especial Missionary prayer meeting, at which the brethren and sisters were commended to the Lord.

June 23. This morning we left for Liverpool, where we safely arrived in the evening.

The following extracts give the account of the Lord's goodness in supplying the necessities of the Orphans, while I was away from Bristol.

On June 25, whilst at Liverpool, I received a letter from brother R. B., master at the Boys'-Orphan-House, dated Bristol, June 24th, in which he writes thus:--The money which you left behind, with 1s. 6d. which came in for Reports, supplied the necessities of yesterday and today; but there is nothing in hand to meet the necessities of tomorrow. Our hope is in God, assuredly believing that He will, as in former times, help us in His own time and manner."--

Two days afterwards the following letter came.

"Bristol, June 26, 1840.

"Dear Brother,--Since I wrote to you we have very sweetly proved the mercy and truth of our heavenly Father, When my letter left Bristol, we had not one penny in hand. On the same evening sister gave me a parcel containing 1l. 1s., the produce of the sale of an article. This was sufficient for yesterday. But after this we were again penniless. I went to the meeting in the evening, where brother J. B. gave me a list of names of persons who had given to him for the Orphans, to the amount of 1l. 4s. 1d. I afterwards sold one of your books, one of brother Craik's Renderings, and a Report. I also remembered that a few days before 2s. 6d. had been given to me which I had forgotten to use. We therefore had in all 1l. 11s. 7d., which is sufficient to meet this day's necessities. I have just received a sovereign for the Orphans, and besides this a box, containing various articles of clothes which has been sent from Wales, part of which articles are only fit for sale. Thus we have something for tomorrow, if needed.

"Your affectionate brother,

"R. B,"

The arrival of the box of clothes, etc., was announced to me in an affectionate letter from a brother in Wales, who sent them, but whom I do not know personally. What follows will show how seasonably the donation came. On June 30th I received another letter from brother B., dated Bristol, June 29th, 1840, in which he writes "I should have posted my letter by one o'clock, but delayed until it was too late, hoping that I might have to speak of the Lord's goodness as well as of our poverty. Thank God, my hopes have been realized!---Besides the 1l. mentioned in my last letter, in the evening of the 26th 11s. 3d. came in for needlework, and 5s. was given. On Saturday I sold some of the clothes which had been sent from Wales for 1l., and 5s. was given to me for an article which had been sold some time ago. As this was scarcely sufficient, I opened the boxes, and found 3s. 2d. in them. The whole, therefore, which was in hand, amounted to 3l. 4s. 5d., which was enough for Saturday the 27th. This morning, Monday, as nothing had been given to me since Saturday, there were no means to provide for the dinner in the Boys'-Orphan-House; but one of the sisters, having a little money of her own, purchased potatoes and meat with it. At eleven o'clock we met for prayer. The baker came to the Infant-Orphan-House, but no bread was taken. A brother left two quarterns of bread at the Boys'-Orphan-House, as a gift. Soon after I received 1l. through sister L. G., which, as soon as I received, I began to write to you. It was a comfort to me, in our poverty, that you still, united in spirit, prayed with us, although distance separated us in body. I do not know that I ever felt more powerfully the kindness of our Heavenly Father, than when I received this last mentioned 1l. Although we are still poor, and soon shall be again in need, yet, receiving it just at this time, it was very refreshing."

The next day I received the following report about the Orphan-Houses from brother B., dated June 30th.--" According to your request, tomorrow only is the time for me to write, but as the Lord has dealt very bountifully with us, I write today, in order that you may be refreshed by the account thereof. Yesterday afternoon, I received 16s., and this morning I sold some more of the articles sent from Wales, for 8s. 6d., which meets this day's demands."

On July 2nd I accompanied the eight German brethren and sisters to the vessel. Just before they went on board, brother ----, one of the missionary brethren, gave me 6l. 10s. for the Orphans. He had sold his plate while at Bristol, considering that as a servant of Jesus Christ, and as one who desired to preach Jesus to the poor Hindoos, he needed it not, This money was the produce of it, except about 2l., which he had spent in purchasing a few books. In giving it to me said, "The money which we have in the common stock, (being altogether 20l. for the eight) is enough for us. For some months, while we are on board, we need no money at all, whilst you may lay it out; and when we need more, the Lord will again supply our need. The other brethren and sisters have no money of their own, and I desire likewise to have none, The Lord has laid the Orphans particularly on my heart, and therefore you must not refuse to accept it."--This brother little knew how on that very day I had been repeatedly asking the Lord for means. Truly this was one of the most remarkable ways of obtaining money, as it came from a poor German missionary, who, in dependence upon the Lord for his temporal supplies, went to the East Indies. I sent off at once 5l. of this money to Bristol. The next day, July 3, I received at Liverpool the following letter from brother B., dated Bristol, July 2nd.--" Since I last wrote, we have still found that the Lord is faithful to His word. May we never be unfaithful towards Him! On Tuesday evening, June 30th, sister C. brought 11s. 6d. for some articles she sold, and I had received 1s. 6d. for Reports. This, with 8s. that had been put into the boxes, met the absolute necessities of yesterday, Wednesday. As nothing has been given since Tuesday, we are, today, Thursday, very needy. I sold the books I mentioned as being sent, with some others which one of the sisters in the Orphan-Houses gave of her own, for 7s., which bought that which was needful for dinner; but there is no money to take in bread nor milk for one of the houses. We met for prayer. Our hope is in God, trusting that He who has so often helped us in poverty, will still do so. If I write any more I shall be too late to post this letter."

[On my return to Bristol I found, which is not mentioned in the next letter, that the milk was purchased with the money of one of the sisters in the Orphan-Houses.]

On July 4th I received the following letter from Bristol, dated July 3rd.

"My dear Brother,--The last account I sent you left us in the greatest poverty. We had sufficient, it is true, for the time then present; but there was no money to take in bread with. In the afternoon there was an old riding habit sent for the Orphans, which I sold this morning for 7s. I also sold a few books for 5s., two old silver thimbles and a ring for 1s. 6d.; besides this, 1s. 6d. was sent for Reports; making in all 15s. This purchased dinner for the three houses. At twelve o'clock we met for prayer. We were indeed in great need. There was no money either for bread or milk. The coals in all the three houses were used, and in every other respect the stores were in a low state. We had really wanted nothing, but there was scarcely any thing left. Well, while we were in prayer to God, your letter came. One of the sisters opened the door and received it, and after prayer it was given to me. You will be able to conceive the greatness of our joy, on opening it, and finding it to contain 5l. I cannot express how much I felt. During the trial I had been much comforted by the Lord's sending a little token of his love every day. It just proved that He was mindful of us in our poverty, and that when His time was come, He would send us an abundance. I think we all felt your absence a little, although not cast down on that account. Money is very precious to those who, like us, so evidently see the HAND and HEART of our Heavenly Father in bestowing it, The sisters send their love to you.

"Your affectionate brother,

"R. B."

On July 6th I received the following account from Bristol, dated July 5th. "You are, I am sure, often praying for us, and therefore see, in the help we receive, God's gracious answers to your prayers, and therefore you will be refreshed by hearing the account of how matters are with us. On Saturday there was again a little money needed in the Girls'-Orphan-House, for butter and such little articles; but I had none in hand, wherewith to supply this need, until nearly tea time, when 5s. was given to me. In the evening of the same day, at ten o'clock, 10s. was sent through brother J. S. You will see that we are still cast simply on God for the future, without anything to depend on but Himself; and on whom, or on what should children depend, but on their most kind Father."

On July 8th, whilst still detained in the Lord's service at Liverpool, I received from a brother 10l. for the Orphans, which I sent off at once. On the same day, after I had sent off the money, I received the following letter from Bristol, dated July 7.

"The Lord is still pleased to keep us very low. Only 4s. 2d. in money has come in since last I wrote to you. The 10s. I told you of, and this 4s. 2d., I divided among the sisters. But as this was far from being sufficient, and knowing that you had received 6l. 10s. and only sent 5l., I took out of the other funds 1l. 6s. 6d., being all that I could spare, and divided it also. I would not have done so, had it not been needful, and had it not appeared to me that we were not going out of the path of obedience in doing this. There was a sack of flour sent this morning. We are still, we may say, in need, as even the money, which I have divided, was not enough to purchase every thing desirable to have."

On July 11th, whilst at Worcester, I received the following letter, dated Bristol, July 9.

"After writing to you the last time, I got no more money on that day, except 1s. The next day, Wednesday, I received 2s. 6d., and took 2s. out of the box in the Boys'-Orphan-House. Also a sister purchased a Bible, and out of that money I took 3s. 6d. to make up the 30s., to which I alluded in my last letter. This carried us through the day. In the evening of the same day I received 11s. 3d. and 2s., which purchased meat for dinner; and the potatoes in the boys' garden, being now fit for use, we had for dinner. After the dinner was provided we received the 10l. from you, which enabled the sisters again to replenish their stock. Out of the 10l. I kept the 30s., in case I might need it on Saturday for the salaries of the masters and governesses of the Day Schools. We felt the poverty a little more, I think, on account of your absence. I knew the Lord would help, but still I felt tried in some measure. The Lord, by His grace, reproves our waywardness towards Him.

When this letter arrived, there was sent to me, at the same time, from Bristol, 5l. for the Orphans, which I sent off at once. On July 17th I returned to Bristol.

I add a few more words respecting my stay at Liverpool.

--About October 1837 I sent some Bibles and 46 copies of my Narrative to a brother in Upper Canada, who, in dependence upon the Lord for temporal supplies, is labouring as a missionary in that country. About eighteen months afterwards I heard, that this box had not arrived. I then wrote to the shipbroker at Liverpool, (who as agent had to send it to America, and to whom I had paid his commission and the freight), to make inquiry about the box; but I received no answer. About a month afterwards my letter was returned to me, through the Dead-Letter Office, and it was stated on the outside that the individual had left Liverpool, and no one knew where he was gone. Putting all these things together, I had now full reason to think that the broker had, never sent off the box. My comfort, however, was, that though this poor sinner had acted thus, yet the Lord, in His own place and way, would use the Bibles and my Narratives. Now, almost immediately after my arrival in Liverpool, a brother told me, that several persons wished to hear me preach who had read my Narrative; and that he knew a considerable number had been bought by a brother, a bookseller, from pawnbrokers, and sold again; and that some also had been ordered from London when there were no more to be had otherwise. It was thus evident that the shipbroker pawned these Narratives before he absconded; but the Lord used them as I had hoped.--I preached ten times in English and once in German whilst at Liverpool, and I know that several persons were brought to hear me, through having read my Narrative.--The German brethren preached twice in German, there being several German vessels in the port, and a number of German sugar refiners living at Liverpool. Liverpool seems to me especially a place where a brother, who is familiar with French and German, may find an abundance of work among the German and French sailors, in the way of preaching to them, and in the way of distributing French and German Bibles and Tracts.--One of the German missionary brethren found out a brother in the Lord, a native of the same town in Prussia, from whence he himself comes, who repeatedly met with us. This dear sailor was the only believer in the vessel in which he was, and has had to suffer much for the Lord's sake.--When the German brethren and sisters were going on board, I engaged a fly for the purpose of taking all their small luggage. When the man put the luggage into the fly, I was struck by its having a hind boot, which I had never seen before in any fly, which he opened, and into which he put several carpet bags. There were seventeen packages altogether. When we arrived at the vessel it was just on the point of going into the river, with several other vessels, and there were crowds of people standing at the docks. The flyman took out the luggage and was on the point of leaving, when I asked him whether he had taken out all the luggage, which I had not been able to count, because of the pressure of people, and the rapidity with which the packages were taken to the vessel. His reply was, Yes. But all at once, by the good hand of God, I remembered the hind boot, and I asked him to open it. The man, somewhat confused, opened it, and in it were five or six carpet bags. This

107

thing showed me afresh our entire dependence upon the Lord, step by step. I was alone. The crowd was great. The vessel was on the point of sailing: and all without my fault or the fault of any one; but it was so through unforseen circumstances. One minute later, and the bags, in all human probability, would have been lost. For when the brethren had missed their luggage, it would have been too late; for though I had marked the number of the fly when I engaged it, yet that would have profited nothing, when once the brethren were at sea. But the hand of God was for good upon these His children, whose stock of linen was only such as they would need. Such a circumstance should teach one to make the very smallest affairs a subject of prayer; for instance, That all the luggage might be safely taken out of a fly.

On July 10th my wife and I left Liverpool, where we had experienced much kindness, for Worcester, where we stayed a few days, and had again much love shown to us by the saints there.

July 25. Since July 11th the Lord has kindly sent in the supplies for the Orphans, so that we have had always something coming in, before the last which was in hand was spent. Now, today, having paid out this morning 8l. 5s., again nothing was left in hand, when in the afternoon 3l. came in by sale of articles.

July 26. Lord's-day. As I had no opportunity today of preaching in our chapels (there being two brethren ministering among us who are strangers in Bristol), I have preached twice this evening in the open air. Precious as this work is, yet I am sure it is not that to which I am called for a constancy, as I have no strength of body for it. But I have seen afresh this evening how greatly it is needed. The second time I preached, I took my stand in a court, filled with poor people, almost every one of whom was dirty, though it was the Lord's day evening. A woman readily lent me a chair on which I stood, and could thus be heard by the people in the houses behind and before me, and on my right and left hand. Judging from their dirty appearance, I should not suppose any of these poor people had been any where, to hear the Gospel preached throughout the day. How plenteous is the harvest, and how few are the labourers! Lord of the harvest, send Thou, in compassion to poor sinners, more labourers into the harvest! --How well a brother who has some gift, and a measure of strength of lungs, might employ a part of the Lord's days, or of other days, either by reading the Scriptures from house to house to such persons, and making some remarks on them; or by standing up in a court and reading the Scriptures aloud and speaking on them. It is very rarely that one meets with decided opposition on these occasions; at least I have generally in such cases found far more readiness to listen, than decidedly to oppose.

Aug. 1. A few days since a brother was staying with me, on his way to his father, whom he had not seen for above two years, and who was greatly opposed to him, on account of the decided steps which his son had taken for the Lord. Before this brother left, that precious promise of our Lord was brought to my mind: "If two of you shall agree on earth as touching any thing that they shall ask, it shall be done for them of my Father which is in heaven." Matt. xviii. 19. Accordingly, I went to the brother's room, and having agreed to pray about a kind reception from his father, and the conversion of both parents, we prayed together.--Today this brother returned. The Lord has answered already one part of the prayer. The brother was most kindly received, contrary to all natural expectation. May the Lord now help us both to look for an answer to the other part of our prayer! There is nothing too hard for the Lord!

Since the publication of the third edition, the father of this brother died. He lived above ten years after Aug. 1, 1840, until he was above 86 years of age; and as he continued a life of much sin and opposition to the truth, the prospect with reference to his conversion became darker and darker. But at last the Lord answered prayer. This aged sinner was entirely changed, simply rested on the Lord Jesus for the salvation of his soul, and became as much attached to his believing son, as before he had been opposed to him; and wished to have him about him as much as possible, that he might read the Holy Scriptures to him and pray with him. Let this instance encourage believers, who have unbelieving parents, to continue in prayer for them.

Since the publication of the fourth edition, the mother also died. About sixteen years had elapsed, after her son and I had thus prayed together, before, in her case, the answer was granted; yet she, too, at last, in very advanced years, was brought to trust in the Lord Jesus alone for the salvation of her soul.--I distinctly remember, with what full assurance, that the Lord would answer our united supplication, I went to the room of this brother, to propose prayer, resting upon the promise in Matt. xviii. 19, though the case appeared to be most hopeless.

Aug. 6. Yesterday I was led, by the sense of our necessity, and the knowledge of the Father's heart, like Elijah, to go again and again to Him with my request for help, as there was nothing in hand for the Orphans to supply the necessities of today. Last evening, after the meeting, a brother from Oxford gave me a sovereign for the Orphans; by two other individuals was sent half-a-crown; and by the sale of an article, which had been given many weeks since, but was only disposed of today, came in 5s.: thus, in all, the Lord sent again 1l. 7s. 6d. This morning I heard that 10s. was given yesterday to brother B., so that we were able to meet the demands of today, which are 1l. 15s.

Aug. 7. As there was only 2s. 6d. in hand, I asked the Lord repeatedly yesterday to send us what was needed for today. When I came home last evening from the meeting, 5l. was given to me, which Q. Q. had brought while I was away, to be used as I thought well. This I took for the Orphans, which will supply our need for today and tomorrow.

Aug. 8. Saturday. This evening I was meditating on the 4th Psalm. The words in verse 3: "But know that the Lord hath set apart him that is godly for Himself; the

Lord will hear when I call upon Him," I was enabled to apply to myself, and they led me to prayer for spiritual blessings. Whilst in prayer, the need of the Orphans (there being now again not one penny in hand), was also brought to my mind, and I asked the Lord respecting this likewise. ABOUT FIVE MINUTES AFTERWARDS I was informed that a sister wished to see me. She brought 1l. 10s. for the Orphans. Thus the Lord has already kindly sent a little to begin the week with. There was also still further given today, 1s. 11d.; and 5s. 1d. was taken out of the boxes in the Orphan-Houses.

Aug. 10. Monday. The 1l. 17s. which came in on Saturday evening for the Orphans, was not enough for the necessities of today, as 2l. 15s. was required. About noon, the Lord gave through a brother in Bath, who has a relative in one of the Orphan-Houses, 1l. 10s. more, so that we had enough, and a few shillings left. This evening came in 4s. besides, also 15s. 6d. by sale of articles.

Aug. 11. The money which was in hand, with 3s. which was given by one of the labourers, as there was not enough otherwise, helped us through this day.

Aug. 12. One of the labourers gave today 10s. of his own, as nothing had come in. Yet this would not have been sufficient, had there not been sold two pairs of stockings, which had been knitted by the boys, for 4s. 1d., and had not 5s. been found in one of the boxes.

Aug. 13. Yesterday there was given a collection of shells, which was sold today, and supplied the necessities of this day, with an addition of 10s. which a brother gave last evening, and 4s. which was taken out of the box in the Infant-Orphan-House.

Aug. 14. There was nothing at all in hand. I opened the box in my house, and found 1s. 4d. in it, A labourer gave 4s. of his own. There was found 1s, 6d. in the boxes in the Orphan-Houses, and 5s. came in by the sale of a few articles which had been given for that purpose. By this 11s. 10d, we were able to meet the absolute need, but were able to take in only a small quantity of bread.

Aug. 15. There was today the greatest poverty in all the three houses; all the stores were very low, as the income throughout the week had been so small. In addition to this it was Saturday, when the wants are nearly double in comparison with other days. At least 3l. was needed to help us comfortably through the day; but there was nothing towards this in hand. My only hope was in God.

The very necessity led me to expect help for this day; for if none had come, the Lord's name would have been dishonoured. Between twelve and one two sisters in the Lord called on me, and the one gave me 2l. and the other 7s. 6d. for the Orphans. With this I went to the Boys'-Orphan-House about one o'clock, where I found the children at dinner. Brother B. put the following note into my hand, which he was just going to send off:

"Dear Brother,--With potatoes from the children's garden, and with apples from the tree in the play-ground (which apples were used for apple dumplings), and 4s. 6d. the price of some articles given by one of the labourers, we have a dinner. There is much needed. But the Lord has provided and will provide."

There came in still further this day by sale of Reports, 1s., by the box in the Girls'-Orphan-House, 1s., by children's needlework, 6s. 6d., by a donation of one of the sisters in the Orphan-Houses, 6s. Thus we had this day 3l. 6s. 6d. to meet all necessities, and are brought to the close of another week.

Aug. 16. Lord's-day. There came in still further last evening, 3s. by sale of some articles, and today 2s. was given, and 5l.; so that the Lord in His love and faithfulness has given us what we are likely to need tomorrow and the day after.

Aug. 17. There has come in still further 2l.

Aug. 18. This morning a brother who passed through Bristol gave 1l., saying that it had been especially laid on his heart to do so. Thus the Lord has provided a little towards tomorrow. Besides this came in today 1s. 9d.

Aug. 19. By the sale of three pairs of stockings came in 5s. 6d., and from Liverpool was sent 12s. 6d.: this, with what was in hand, was enough for today, and left a little over.

Aug. 20. Today there was not enough money in hand to meet all the demands; but it being known that yesterday several persons had put money into the boxes in the Orphan-Houses, they were opened, and found to contain 1l. 4s. 6d., which was more than sufficient.

I would call upon the believing reader to admire the love and wisdom and power of God in ordering it so that persons should come to the Orphan-Houses just at the time when there is temporal pressure, and should be influenced to put money into the boxes. These little sums have been often the means of helping us in our greatest need. The especial providence of God, as in every other respect, so in this particular point also, is to be seen respecting this Institution, in that so much is anonymously put into the boxes; for there has been no less than 45l. 18s. 9 3/4d. put in during the last two years, from Dec. 10, 1838, to Dec. 10, 1840.

Aug. 22. Saturday. Yesterday there was only 13s. 6d. in hand, which was enough to meet the necessities of the day, but not sufficient to enable us to take in the usual quantity of bread. This morning we were in much need, not only because there were no means for procuring dinner in the Boys' and Girls'-Orphan-Houses, but also because, this being Saturday, we had to procure provisions for two days. When brother B. went to the Infant-Orphan-House, to make inquiry about the demands for today, he was informed that money had been put into the box there, which was found to be 12s. There came in also in the morning 10s, besides. This 1l. 2s. was more than sufficient to purchase all that was needed for dinner. Between twelve and one o'clock there arrived a parcel from Clapham, which contained several donations for the Orphans, amounting to 2l. 15s., besides a pair of sheets and pillow cases, 4 frocks, 4 handkerchiefs, 4 caps, 1 stuff petticoat, 2 chemises, 6 bags, 1 little shirt, (all new), and several yards of prints and calico. In the evening came a box from Worcester, which contained the following articles for sale: a valuable veil, 2 silver ladles, a silver fork, 2 pairs of new plated candlesticks, a fan, and 2 Italian books. There came also from the neighbourhood of Wolverhampton, 2s. 6d. and seven books. Thus the Lord helped us through this day also, at the commencement of which we were so very poor, and needed several pounds.

Aug. 23. Lord's-day. As we have often found it to be the case, so it is again now. After the Lord has tried our faith, He, in the love of His heart, gives us an abundance, to show that not in anger, but for the glory of His name, and for the trial of our faith He has allowed us to be poor. This morning I received from an aged and afflicted servant, 3l.; and a little afterwards 8l. from Q. Q. From another servant 5s.; also 2s. was put anonymously into the box at Bethesda, besides the 1l. 10s. for rent. Thus the Lord has kindly given today 12l. 17s.

Aug. 29. Saturday. Since last Monday had come in only 2l. by the profits of the sale of ladies' baskets, 1l. 14s. 10d. by sale of articles, 3s. as two donations, and 6d. by Reports. Thus it happened that when this day began, though a Saturday, we had only 7s. in hand. In the course of the morning came in 11s. 9d., and towards the evening 8s. 6d. This day we have been as poor in regard to our stores, as at any time. During the whole of this day, though Saturday, we had only 1l. 7s. 3d, On this account we had to buy a smaller quantity of bread than usual, etc.; nevertheless the children have even this day lacked nothing, and there is a sufficient quantity of wholesome food till breakfast on Monday morning.

For many weeks past very little has come in for the other funds. The chief supply has been by the sale of Bibles. Last Saturday I was not able to pay the whole of the weekly salaries of the teachers in the Day Schools, which, however, does not make me a debtor to them, as it is an understood thing, that they have not to look to me for payment, but to the Lord. Today again only 2s. was in hand, whilst several pounds were needed to pay the salaries. It appeared now plainly to be the will of the Lord that, as all the labourers in the Orphan-Houses know about the state of the funds, so the brethren and sisters who labour in the Day Schools should share the trial of faith and the joy of faith with us. Accordingly we all met, and after I had laid on their hearts, the importance of keeping to themselves, for the Lord's sake, the state of the funds, we prayed together.

Aug. 30. Lord's day. Today the Lord has again bountifully opened His hand for the Orphans. There came in with Ecclesiastes ix. 10, 5l.; from a sister, a servant, 10s.; and for rent 1l. 10s. Besides this, was anonymously put into the box at Bethesda, 10s. 3d. and 2s. 6d.

Sept. 1. Though there was a good supply given to the matrons yesterday, yet, as the stock of provisions had been so low on Saturday, the money was all spent by last evening; and had the Lord not kindly sent in yesterday 14s., and today 1l. 10s., we should have been again in need.

Sept. 4. The day before yesterday, Sept. 2, came a box from Leeds, from sisters in the Lord whom we have never seen, and of whom until now we have never heard, but on whose hearts the Lord has laid His work in our hands. The box contained a variety of articles, to be sold for the benefit of the Orphans. No money has come in the last two days, except 1s. which was given, and 5s. for things sold. On this account the boxes in the Orphan-Houses were opened, but only 1s. 7 1/2d. was found in them. To supply what was needed today, an article which came in the box from Leeds was sold for 5s. and thus we were helped through the day. The sisters who sent the box from Leeds wrote to us a most affectionate letter, in which they announced this and another box which is to follow, stating how much the Lord had laid the work in our hand on their hearts. They may have little thought, when they sent off the box, that so soon the produce of one of the articles sent by them would supply our need.

Sept. 5. Saturday. Because there had come in so little during the last days, at least 3l. was requisite to supply the need of today. There was, however, not one penny in hand when the day commenced. Last evening the labourers in the Orphan-Houses, together with the teachers of the Day Schools, met for prayer. This morning one of the teachers, who had a little money of his own, brought 1l. 5s. 6d. Thus, as we had hoped, we were enabled to provide for the dinner. In the afternoon all of us met again for prayer. Another teacher of the Day Schools gave 2s, 6d, and 1s. came in besides. But all this was not enough. There was no dinner provided for tomorrow, nor was there any money to take in milk tomorrow, and besides this a number of other little things were to be purchased, that there might be no real want of anything. Now observe how our kind father helped us! Between seven and eight this evening a sister, whose heart the Lord has made willing to take on her the service of disposing of the articles which are sent for sale, brought 2l. 10s. 6d. for some of the things which came a fortnight ago from Worcester, and last Wednesday from Leeds. The sister stated, that though she did not feel at all well, she had come because she had it so laid on her heart, that she could not stay away. Our Father knew our need, and therefore, though so late, He sent this help. Thus we were richly provided with all we needed this Saturday.

Sept. 6. The Lord has kindly sent in today for the Orphans 4l. 5s. 6d. for the need of tomorrow. One pound of this money was given by a servant, who has again and again given of late, and who has thus again and again been the means of supplying our need, when there was either nothing at all, or not sufficient in hand. When she gave me the money to-night, she told me that of late she had had the Orphans particularly laid on her heart. 1l. 3s. was the produce of an orphan-box, which a sister was led so seasonably to send just now.

Sept. 7. This morning a brother from Barnstaple, who came on Saturday evening (that evening when we were so greatly tried, but so graciously delivered), gave me 1l. 0s. 3d., which the love of some saints at Barnstaple had sent for the Orphans, besides 5s. of his own. We have thus enough for today and tomorrow. There came in still further today, 6s. 6d.

Sept. 8. How kindly has the Lord so ordered it that for some time past the income for the school-fund should have been so little, in order that thus we might be constrained to let the labourers in the Day Schools share our joys and our trials of faith, which had been before kept from them! But as above two years ago the Lord ordered it so that it became needful to communicate to the labourers in the Orphan-Houses the state of the funds, and made it a blessing to them, so that I am now able to leave Bristol, and yet the work goes on, so, I doubt not, the brethren and sisters who are teachers in the Day Schools will be greatly blessed by being thus partakers of our precious secret respecting the state of the funds. Our prayer meetings have already been a blessing to us, and united us more than ever in the work. We have them now every morning at seven, and we shall continue them, the Lord helping us, till we see His hand stretched forth, not merely in giving us means for the teachers, but also for other purposes; for we need a stove in one of the school rooms, a fresh supply of several kinds of Bibles and New Testaments, and it is desirable to have means to help Missionary brethren who labour in dependence upon the Lord for the supply of their temporal necessities.

Sept. 9. We are now meeting every morning at seven for prayer. With 5s. which was sent yesterday from the Isle of Wight for the Orphans, we have commenced the day; but I believe that the Lord will help us through this day also.

Evening. About twelve this morning a brother, a stranger, who is staying at Ashton, near Bristol, came with some of his family to the Orphan-Houses. While brother B. was for a few moments out of the room to fetch a key, the visiting brother took the opportunity of secretly putting something into the box at the Boys'-Orphan-House. Brother B., however, perceived it before he could get away from the box, and, the brother being gone, our great need brought it out, when it was found to be 5l. Thus the Lord kindly has provided for the need of today and tomorrow. When this money was given we were exceedingly poor. For not only would there have been no means to take in the usual quantity of bread in one of the houses, but there was no money to take in milk in the afternoon in any of the houses. The Lord knew our need, and therefore just now sent this brother. He gave also 2s. for Reports.

Sept. 10. When now the 5l. of yesterday was again spent, the Lord has kindly sent another 5l. There came in still further 6s. 10d.

Yesterday came in it. 7s., and today 1l. 15s. 10d. for the other funds. Thus the Lord, in answer to our petitions at the morning prayer meetings, has sent in a little for these funds also.

Sept. 11. The Lord has sent in still further and more richly for the Orphans. This morning 1l. was given to me which had been sent from Trowbridge, and this afternoon a brother who came from Scotland gave me 10l., and brought the following trinkets which were sent by a lady from Scotland:--2 clasps, a ring, 2 pairs of ear-rings, a slide, a pin, a cross, and 2 bracelets, all of gold. In the afternoon came in 3l. by sale of articles.

Sept. 12. The Lord has sent in still more. This morning was sent 10l. through a banker in London, by the order of a sister at Worcester; and 10s. was put into the box at my house. This has been a week of peculiar mercies, as above 40l. has been sent in, besides several articles. We have continued to meet for prayer every morning, from seven to eight.

Sept. 13. Today came in 3l. 8s. 4d.,of which 1l. 10s. 6d. was for some of the articles sent from Leeds.

Sept. 16. Though during the last week above 40l. came in, yet, because the usual expenses for housekeeping were about 15l., and because most of the sisters who labour in the Orphan-Houses had not had for a long time any money for their own personal necessities, we were the day before yesterday again so poor, that only a few shillings were left. The Lord, knowing this, sent in a little money, and, by a sister from the Isle of Wight, 7 rings, 2 brooches, 2 pins, 1 pair of ear-rings, 2 pairs of studs, all of gold, 2 chemises, and 2 babies' shirts. Today arrived from Leeds, from two sisters in the Lord before referred to, a second box, the first having come about a fortnight ago. This second box contained the following articles:--2 silver dessert spoons, a pair of silver sugar tongs, a silver tea caddy spoon, 6 plated forks, 4 knife resters, a cream spoon, 6 Britannia metal tea spoons, a silver watch, a metal watch, a small telescope, 2 cloak fastenings, 11 pencils, a pen case with pieces of sealing wax, 2 pairs of scissors, 6 chimney ornaments, a boa ring, a chess board, 3 purses with 2l. 1s. 4d., 2 silver pocket knives, a silver pencil case, a ditto of brass, a bodkin case, a gold pin, a silver vinaigrette, 125 needles, 1 memorandum case, 5 paper baskets, 18 books, 100 copies of a small English Grammar (unbound), 75 pamphlets, 37 table mats, 120 little tracts, 5 pairs of stockings, 2 pairs of socks, a Thibet shawl, 6 coloured frocks, 4 caps, 9 collars, 8 neckerchiefs, 3 muslin aprons, 5 holland aprons,

4 muslin frocks, 6 babies' ditto, 2 white gowns, 2 remnants of print, 5 habit shirts, a bonnet, a merino apron, a glass trumpet, a taper candlestick, several small pieces of riband and gauze, 4 yards of silk fringe, 7 cases of different kinds of cards, a crape scarf, some lining calico, 13 little boxes, a straw basket, and about 50 other various little articles. It is difficult to describe the peculiar pleasure which I had in unpacking the box, and in finding that all these articles were for the Lord's work.--There came in still further this evening 8s.

Besides other small donations since the 10th, there came into day 5l. for the other funds, as the answer to oft-repeated prayer; also, from Liverpool, 1l. 14s. 8d. Thus the Lord encourages our hearts in this part of the work likewise.

Sept. 17. The need of today for the Orphans was supplied by the little which had come in yesterday, and by the 2l. 1s. 4d. which came in the second box from Leeds. These two boxes from Leeds have been sent most seasonably by the Lord, and thus truly the sisters who sent them have been led by Him to do so, according to what they wrote in a letter, which announced the arrival of the first box; "We feel deeply interested in your concerns, and our anxiety to serve you has increased by every new discovery of the kindness and goodness of God, in providing for your wants. Indeed, we cannot but believe that the Lord has put it into our hearts to help you, and we trust you will honour us, His unworthy servants, by believing that our gift is really His." There came in today 2l. 16s. by the sale of some of the articles sent in the first box from Leeds, and by the sale of some other articles. Thus our need for tomorrow is supplied.

Sept. 18. Today the Lord has sent again 17s. 5d. by sale of some of the articles sent from Leeds, and 2l. 10s. from Leicestershire, and also 4s. for children's needlework. Thus we had enough for tomorrow, being Saturday.

Sept. 21. Monday. By what was in hand for the Orphans, and by what had come in yesterday, the need of today is more than supplied, as there is enough for tomorrow also.

Today a brother from the neighbourhood of London gave me 10l., to be laid out as it might be most needed. we have been praying many days for the School- Bible--and Missionary Funds, I took it all for them. This brother knew nothing about our work, when he came three days since to Bristol. Thus the Lord, to show His continued care over us, raises up new helpers. They that trust in the Lord shall never be confounded! Some who helped for a while may fall asleep in Jesus; others may grow cold in the service of the Lord; others may be as desirous as ever to help, but have no longer the means; others may have both a willing heart to help, and have also the means, but may see it the Lord's will to lay them out in another way;--and thus, from one cause or another, were we to lean upon man, we should surely be confounded; but, in leaning upon the living God alone, We are BEYOND

116

disappointment, and BEYOND being forsaken because of death, or want of means, or want of love, or because of the claims of other work. How precious to have learned in any measure to stand with God alone in the world, and yet to be happy, and to know that surely no good thing shall be withheld from us whilst we walk uprightly!

Sept. 23. This morning there was again only 10s. in hand for the Orphans. As this was not enough for the day, I opened the box in my house, in which I found 8s. 6d. The boxes in the Orphan-Houses were also opened, which contained 7s. 6 1/2d. There came in also by the sale of a pair of stockings, 1s. 6d. This 1l., 7s. 6 1/2d. was enough, and even 3s. more than was absolutely needed. The Lord gave today another proof that He is still mindful of us, for a brother sent half a ton of coals to each of the three houses.

Sept. 24. Yesterday our prayer, in our meeting at twelve o'clock, was especially for the supply of today. I was fully assured that the Lord would send help, as now all our stores were again exhausted. Accordingly, last evening a sister, into whose hands some of the articles, which came in the second box from Leeds, had been put for sale, gave me 1l. 3s. 7d., being the payment for some of them. There came in a donation of 2s. besides. This 1l. 5s. 7d. served for this day. The Lord be praised who has helped us thus!

Sept. 25. It is now half-past eleven. Nothing has come in as yet. How the Lord will help us through the day is not my care; for sure I am He will help. I am just going to meet with my fellow-labourers for prayer. Perhaps the Lord will again, at the time of the meeting, fill our mouths with praise, as He has done so many times. My soul waits on Him for deliverance! How truly precious to have such a Father as we have!

Sept. 26. When I went yesterday to the meeting for prayer, I found that some articles, which had come from Leeds, had been sold for 10s. 9d., and that 2s. 6d. had been taken out of the box in the Girls'-Orphan-Ho use. To this one of the labourers added 10s. of his own. This 1l. 3s. 3d. supplied all we needed yesterday; but there was now again nothing in hand to meet this day's demands, which I knew would be great, on account of its being Saturday. The Lord, however, remembered our Saturday's necessities, and therefore sent in abundantly, so that we had even more than we needed for today, though we required no less than 5l. The way in which He kindly helped us, was this: first, 3l. came in for articles which had been sent from Leeds; afterwards a little boy and girl brought two little Savings' Banks, filled with their little presents, amounting altogether to 15s 1 1/4d. In the evening came in still further 4l. for articles which had been sold, most of which had likewise been sent from Leeds. Thus the Lord sent in altogether 8l. 18s. 1 1/4d. in the course of the day, whilst it commenced without there being a penny in hand.

Sept. 27. Today the Lord has sent in still further 2l. 5s. 8d., of which 15s. 8d. was for articles sent from Leeds, and 1l. with Ecclesiastes ix. 10.

Sept. 29. Yesterday we were again penniless, after the necessities of the three houses had been supplied. Almost immediately afterwards came in 1l. 12s. 2d., sufficient to supply the need of today.

Sept. 30. Today there is nothing in hand. It is now a quarter past eleven, but nothing yet has come in. Nevertheless the Lord will surely help us this day also! About five minutes after I had written the above, I was informed by a note from brother B., that 2l. 10s. 6d. had come in in small donations.

Oct. 1. It is now again eleven o'clock, and the Lord has not as yet been pleased to send in any thing for the necessities of this day. Let me see now how the Lord will again help us in the love of His heart; for He will surely help, though I know not how.--Evening. When I went to the prayer meeting, I found that only 1s. had come in, but at the same time I was informed that the money, which had been divided yesterday among the matrons, was enough for today also.

Oct. 2. Nothing came in yesterday, nor this morning. In addition to this, I was so engaged, that in the afternoon I had not even time to make inquiry how the Lord had helped. Thus it is often that I can do nothing but quietly go on with my engagements, casting all care upon the Lord. When I came home this evening, the first thing that met my eyes was the following letter from a distance of many miles:

"Beloved Brother,--Five pounds are enclosed as from the Lord, as I believe you stand in need of it for the use of the Orphans. Yours affectionately, F. W.

Truly, the Lord, to whom we had spoken yesterday, had spoken for us, and told this brother that we were in need of money. After having read this letter, my eyes met two others. In the one I was informed by a brother, that he had sold two pairs of fire screens for 8s., and had sent the money. These screens had been for many months in his hands for sale, and now to-day, in this our poverty, a lady came to the shop and bought them. The other letter was from brother B., master of the boys in the Boys'-Orphan-House, which I give here:

"I opened the boxes and found 4s. 1 1/2d. in them. This was far from being sufficient. About four o'clock three persons came to the Orphan-Houses, and put into the box at the Boys'-Orphan-House 7s., into the box at the Infant-Orphan-House 6s., and into the box at the Girls'-Orphan-House 7s. Thus I have had in all to divide 1l. 4s. 1 1/2d., which meets the necessities of the day."

Oct. 3. It was exceedingly kind of the Lord to send in so much yesterday; for the necessities of today, being Saturday, required it all. And now, when there was again nothing in hand, there arrived this evening a large box, sent by a sister at Stafford, whom I never saw, which contained 1l. 5s., and the following articles: 11 gold rings, a silver ring washed, a locket, a gold brooch, 3 single ear-rings, a watch hook, a silver watch-guard, 2 silver-mounted eye glasses, 3 vinaigrettes, 2 purses, a silver buckle, 2 old silver coins, 2 silver pencil cases, 3 pairs of bracelets, 3 necklaces, 2 waist buckles, a bracelet snap, a cloak fastening, a necklace snap, a yard measure, a mourning brooch, 7 pincushions, a snuff box, a small looking glass, 2 china boxes, a china inkstand, 5 china cups and saucers, a china basket, 2 china jugs, a scent bottle, a boa ring, 20 shells, a boy's cap, a pair of snuffers and stand, a little basket, a pair of screen handles, 3 ornamental pens, 5 artificial flowers, 5 glass plates, 5 counter plates, 3 pairs of card racks, a comb, a pair of watch pockets, 12 table mats, 8 paintings, 4 drawings, 2 fans, a pair of garters, 3 pairs of gloves, 3 pairs of silk stockings, 3 veils, a gauze scarf, 6 ladies' bags, 5 silk bands, 2 floss silk scarfs, a gauze handkerchief, 2 silk scarfs, a crape shawl, a silk shawl, 2 muslin capes, 30 yards of worn cotton lace, 8 yards of muslin work, 9 yards of print, a pinafore, a frock, a sampler, a pair of socks, a pair of ear-rings, and 17 ladies' dresses.--One thing is particularly to be noticed respecting this donation, that the Lord from time to time raises up fresh individuals to help us in the work, thereby continually reminding us, that He is not limited to any individuals in particular, neither are we, His children.

Oct. 4. Today came in 19s. 4d., by sale of some of the articles sent from Leeds. Thus our need for tomorrow is supplied.

Oct. 5. 7l. 15s. 2d. came in again today, of which 5l. was from a brother whom I have never seen.

Oct. 6. Today came in further by sale of articles which had been sent from Leeds, 3l. 7s. 6d., also 14s. 3d. in small donations.

Oct. 7. 1l. 14s. 2d. came in today in small donations.

It is now five weeks, since we have daily met for prayer. Not indeed merely to ask for means, but for grace and wisdom for ourselves in reference to the work, for the conversion of the children under our care, for grace for those children who stand already on the Lord's side, for a blessing upon the circulation of the Scriptures, for a blessing upon the work, with reference to the church at large, etc. But whilst we thus, as the Spirit led us, prayed for various things, nevertheless the lack of means was that which had brought us day after day together. We asked the Lord to give us the means which are needed for carrying on the Day Schools, for buying Bibles, as several sorts are needed, and to enable us to assist Missionary work in foreign countries. Never at any previous time, since first the work commenced on March 5, 1834, have we had to continue so long a time in prayer for these funds, without obtaining the answer. The Lord, however, gave us grace to "continue in prayer," and keep our hearts in the assurance that He would help. Now, though He delayed long, before He sent us the answer, in His own time He made it manifest, that He had not only not shut His ear against our prayer in anger, but that He had answered them even before we called; for there was sent today, from the East Indies, a bank order for 100l., which had been sent off two months since, therefore several days before we even began to pray. It was left to me to apply this money as it might be needed. As we had so long, and so particularly prayed for these funds, I took the whole of it for them, and not for the Orphan-Fund. --The Lord be praised for this precious answer. It was particularly precious, as leading the dear brethren and sisters who labour in the Day Schools, and who comparatively are little accustomed to this way, to see how good it is to wait upon the Lord.

Oct. 10. All our wants for the Orphans have been richly supplied during this week; and today, on my leaving for Trowbridge in the Lord's service, I was able to send 5l. 5s. 8d. to the sisters, the matrons.

Oct. 11--14. Trowbridge. I have had a good season since I have been here. The Lord has enabled me to rise very early, and I have thus had more than two hours of communion with Him before breakfast, the fruit of which I have felt all the day long. The Lord in mercy continue my enjoyment!--For the last three weeks I had been asked, yea pressed, to come here, to minister among the saints; but I could not clearly see it to be the Lord's will, and therefore did not go. Now I came, assured that it was His will, and have been very happy, and greatly helped in my service here in every way, and I am fully assured that my labour has not been in vain. How good it is, even for this life, according to the Lord's bidding either to go or stay!--I have seen, whilst here, a young woman, the daughter of a brother and sister who were in communion with us, but who have both fallen asleep. While her father was living she hated the truth, but still she came to Bethesda Chapel. One day, whilst there, she was made to feel the power of the truth: and, since the death of her parents, the Lord has granted an answer to their many prayers on her behalf; for she is now standing on the Lord's side. Let believing parents continue in prayer for their children, and let them also continue affectionately and at suitable times to bring the truth before them, and to bring them to the preaching of the Word: and in due season it will be manifested that their labours were not in vain.

Oct. 14. Yesterday, while at Trowbridge, I received from a sister, from the neighbourhood of London, 1l. for the Orphans. In the evening, a sister, a servant, gave me 1s. This morning I gave myself again to prayer respecting the Orphan-Fund, as I had reason to believe that there was nothing in hand in Bristol, except several pounds had come in since I left. Soon after, a sister, a servant, gave me 5s., and, on leaving in the afternoon, a brother gave me 5l. When I came home this evening, I found that only 3l. 10s. 8d. had come in since I left, just sufficient to supply the need up to this evening, so that the help which the Lord gave at Trowbridge, in answer to prayer, came very seasonably to supply the need of tomorrow.

Oct. 20. Tuesday. During these last three days we have again experienced the continued care of our loving Father on behalf of the Orphans. On Saturday evening, when again there was no money at all remaining in my hands, a pair of silver mounted horns was anonymously left at my house. On the Lord's day I received 6l. 1s. Yesterday the Lord sent in still more abundantly; for in the morning came in 12l. from the neighbourhood of Wolverhampton, and in the evening 2l. was given to me by D. C. This morning, a few minutes after I had been thinking that no potatoes had been sent yet for the Orphans, and that we had no money to lay in a stock (for the 14l. which came in yesterday was at once sent off), a brother came and informed me that he had given orders that twenty sacks of good potatoes should be sent to the Orphan-Houses. Thus our kind Father continually cares for us.

Oct. 26. Monday. The Lord has been again very kind to us, during these last days. There came in since Oct. 20, in small donations, 18s. 1d.; for knitting and by sale of stockings, 16s. On Friday last, besides, there were sold stockings to the amount of 17s. 5d. In the evening a brother gave me 5l. This 5l. and the money for the stockings came in very seasonably, as it enabled us to supply the large demands of the next day. Yesterday morning, when I took my hat from the rail, I found in one of my gloves a note, containing a 5l. note and the following words: "2l. for the Orphans, the rest for dear brother and sister Muller," There came in still further yesterday 2l. 12s. 6d. Thus we are again supplied for about three days.

In reference to the note which was put into my hat, containing 5l., I just add, that I had repeatedly asked the Lord for means for our own personal expenses, previous to the reception of it, as we had but very little money for ourselves. Indeed the very moment, before I took my hat from the rail, I had risen from my knees, having again asked the Lord for means for ourselves and for the Orphans.

Oct. 30. The evening before last 9s. came in, being the produce of some work which a sister had done for the benefit of the Orphans; and early this morning, while my candle was yet burning, a paper was brought, containing 12s. These two donations, with what little is in hand besides, supply our need for this day.

Oct. 31. Saturday. There was no money in hand, My mind was particularly stirred up to open the box in my house. I did so, and found 1l. 10s. 7d. in it. The boxes in the Orphan-Houses were likewise opened, in which was found 8s. Also a brother from Tetbury gave 2s. 6d. Thus the need of today was supplied.

Nov. 2. Monday. 1l. 11s, is the need of today, and as 1l. 12s. has come in since Saturday evening, we are helped for today.

November 3 and 4. Only 2s. 6d. has come in since Nov. 2nd, but the necessities of these two days were supplied by means of articles which had been given to be disposed of.

Nov. 5. Only 2s. came in yesterday for knitting. We are now, without any thing, cast upon the Lord. The need of today is 1l. 3s., which I am unable to send.-- Afternoon. There came in at three o'clock 4l. for some of the articles which had been sent from Stafford, and which had been sold some time since, so that I was able to send the needful supplies. There came in 6d. besides.

Nov. 7. Saturday. Of the 4l. 2s. 6d. which was in hand the day before yesterday, there was so much left, that, with an addition of 9s. 6d., all the necessities of today could be supplied. This one of the labourers gave.

Nov. 8. Lord's day. Today the Lord has been again very kind, and looked upon us in our poverty. Besides the 1l. 10s. for rent, I received with Ecclesiastes ix. 10, 5l. I was also informed that two large sacks of oatmeal had been sent from Glasgow as a present. In addition to all this, a brother told me that he had it in his heart to give 10l. worth of materials, for winter clothes for the children, leaving the material to my choice, according to the need, so that just what was most desirable might be given. (He, accordingly, sent a few days after, a large pair of good blankets, 32 1/2 yards of mixed beaver, and 10 1/2 yards of blue beaver for cloaks.) There was also 1s. put into the box at Bethesda, with the words, "Jehovah Jireh." These words have often been refreshing to my soul for many years past, and I wrote them with a valuable diamond ring, set with ten brilliants, which was given to the Orphans about twenty months since, upon a pane of glass in my room, which circumstance, in remembrance of the remarkable way in which that valuable ring came, has often cheered my heart, when in deep poverty my eyes have been cast upon "JEHOVAH JIREH"(i.e. the Lord will provide) whilst sitting in my room.

I purposed to have gone to Trowbridge yesterday, and had settled it so on Friday evening with brother ----. But no sooner had I decided to do so, than I felt no peace in the prospect of going. After having prayed about it on Friday evening, and yesterday morning, I determined not to go, and I felt sure the Lord had some reason for not allowing me to feel happy in the prospect of going. I began now to look out for blessings for this day, considering that the Lord had kept me here for good to some souls. This evening I was especially led to press the truth on the consciences of the unconverted, entreating and beseeching them, and telling them also that I felt sure, the Lord had, in mercy to some of them, kept me from going to Trowbridge. I spoke on Genesis vi. 1--5. Immediately after I saw fruit of the Word. An individual fully opened his heart to me. I walked about with him till about ten o'clock, even as long as I had any strength left. [About ten days afterwards a brother told me of a poor drunkard who heard me that evening, and who since then had stayed up till about twelve o'clock every night to read the Scriptures, and who had not been intoxicated since.]

Nov. 11. As only 4s. 6d. had come in for knitting, and 2s. 6d. as a donation for the Orphans since the 8th, we were now again very poor. Today there was 9s. more needed than there was in hand, which one of the labourers gave. There were sent today anonymously, nine sacks of potatoes, a proof that our Father continues to be mindful of us, though we are now again so poor.

Nov. 12. Only 6s. 6d. came in last night, 4s. 6d. of which is the produce of the work of a sister, and 2s. from a poor afflicted sister. This 6s. 6d. was very precious in my esteem, because it showed me afresh our Father's heart towards us, and it was a little to begin the day with. No more has come in this morning, when at twelve I heard from the Orphan-Houses that 1s. 6d. had been received for knitting, and that about eleven this morning a sovereign was left, anonymously, at the Girls'-Orphan House. The paper in which the sovereign was enclosed contained only the letters "A. U. S."--This was a precious deliverance. We have thus enough for today.--Evening. There came in still further today for knitting 3s., and a little girl sent 1s. When I came home this evening, I found that a boy's jacket and a sovereign had been left anonymously at my house. Truly, these deliverances today have been very precious! We have now enough for tomorrow also.

Nov. 14. Trowbridge. Saturday. That which came in the evening before last supplied our need yesterday; but since then nothing has been received, and therefore there were no means to meet this day's demands. I had to go this morning in the Lord's service to Trowbridge, feeling assured that His time had now come for my going, and it required indeed looking at the power, wisdom, and love of our Father, comfortably to leave my dear fellow-labourers, there being nothing in hand. My comfort was that the same kind Father who had provided would provide.

Nov. 16. Trowbridge. Monday. This morning I received a letter from Bristol, in which I was informed that on Saturday came in 12s. 6d; also 9s. was given by one of the labourers. Besides this were received 3s. by sale of articles, and three small donations, amounting to 5s. Thus the Lord most mercifully sent in 1l. 9s. 6d., which was enough to supply the absolute need.

Nov. 17. Trowbridge. This morning I had again the report from Bristol about yesterday, in order that, though unable to send means, I might help with my prayers. In a note written in the morning by brother B., and sent to my wife, he writes thus: "I know not whether the Lord has sent in any money for the Orphans or not. I have received none. Sister ---- (one of the labourers) has given half a ton of coals to the Boys'-Orphan-House.

There are coals needed at the Girls'-Orphan-House, and much money for the ordinary expenses. There is sufficient in all the houses for dinner. He has said, 'I will never leave thee nor forsake thee,' so that we may boldly say, the Lord is MY helper." In the afternoon of the same day he writes: "I have delayed writing as long as I could. The Lord has not sent any thing, but the sisters can do without taking in bread, and they had money enough to pay for the milk, except sister ----, who has, however, received a few shillings for some articles of her own, that she sold. Thus we are supplied with the absolute necessities for today." In reference to the last lines I make a few remarks. At first sight it might appear as if it were a failure of the principles on which we act, that now and then individuals who are connected with the work have been obliged to sell articles of their own to procure things which were needed. But let it be remembered, that under no circumstances prayer for temporal supplies can be expected to prevail with the Lord, except we are willing to part with money or any needless articles which we may have of our own. Indeed an Institution like the one under my care should not be carried on by any rich believer, on the principles on which we, by grace, are enabled to act, except it be that he were made willing himself to give of his own property, as long as he has any thing, whenever the Institution is in real need.

Nov. 18. Bristol. This morning at twelve I returned from Trowbridge, where I had been very happy, and where the Lord evidently used me this time. How happy a thing it is to go and to stay with the Lord!--I found that yesterday some money had been put into the orphan-box at my house, which my wife had reason to believe was at least 1l. She therefore sent 1l. which had come in for the rent of the Orphan-Houses, in consideration of this, as she had not the key to the box. This 1l. met the necessities of yesterday, and with 1s. additional, which one of the labourers gave, was also enough for the dinner of today. There came in also yesterday from Clapham, as a token that the Lord allows us only to be poor for the trial of our faith, but not in anger, the following articles of clothing: 6 frocks, 7 pinafores, 4 chemises, 3 pocket handkerchiefs, 2 petticoats, 3 night caps, 4 work bags (all new) a yard of merino, and 12 silk papers. On my arrival at home I opened the box in my house, in which I found 2l. 0s. 6d., so that I had 1l. 0s. 6d. to send off, whereby the usual quantity of bread could be taken in.

Nov. 19. Since Sept. 18, 1838, this has been, perhaps, of all the days the most trying. The poverty has been exceedingly great for the last six days. There had come in no money since yesterday. On this account no bread could be taken in, as far as the natural prospect went. Nor was there any money at three in the afternoon to take in milk for tea, when brother B. came to me. However, we prayed together, and the Lord had mercy. For one of the labourers found that he was able, which he knew not before, to give of his own 10s., so that there were the means to take in the milk, by the time that it is usually brought. This evening about six there came in still further 10s. 3d. by the sale of Reports. Thus, by the good hand of our God upon us, we were able to take in bread as usual. How very kind of the Lord that He sent us an abundance of potatoes and two large sacks of oatmeal, before this season of deep poverty, as to pecuniary means, commenced! May the Lord now in great pity look upon us, for we are in deeper poverty than ever, as with every day it increases, whilst there is no full deliverance. Thanks be to the Lord that my mind has been in peace this day also, though our faith has been so very much tried! Thanks to Him that my mind is in peace now, though there is nothing but want on every side before me, respecting tomorrow! Surely, the Lord will again, in His own time, more fully stretch forth His helping hand!

Nov. 20. Nothing more had come in this morning. It was nearly three o'clock this afternoon, when brother B. called on me, to see whether any thing had come in; but I had received nothing. I was obliged to go out with a brother from Devonshire, and therefore requested him to wait till I returned. About a quarter past three I came back, when, among several persons who were waiting at my house to converse with me, there was a sister whom I much desired to see about some church affair. I did so. When I had ended the conversation with her, about half-past three, she gave me 10l. for the Orphans. More sweet, and more needed, were none of the previous deliverances. Language cannot express the real joy in God which I had. I was free from, excitement. The circumstance did not un-fit me even for a single moment to attend to my other engagements. I was not in the least surprised, because, by grace, my soul had been waiting on God for deliverance. Never had help been so long delayed. In none of the houses was milk for tea, and in one even no bread, and there was no money to purchase either. It was only a few minutes before the milkman came, when brother B. arrived at the Orphan-Houses with the money. Yet even now it was more than an hour before the usual tea time. The Lord be praised for this deliverance! Such a week of deep poverty, as we have had since Nov. 13, we never had before. Yet, thanks to the Lord! we have lacked nothing, and we have been kept from dishonouring Him by unbelief. I further notice respecting this day, that before this 10l. was received there was sent to the Infant-Orphan-House a cart load of clumps of wood, when there were neither coals, nor money to buy any.

Nov. 21. Saturday evening. The 10l. which came in yesterday afternoon is all expended. Again I have not a penny in hand. We are, however, brought to the close of another week, and have now, a little at least, replenished our provision stock; and should the Lord permit us to enter upon another week, He will surely provide according to our need.

Nov. 22. Lord's day. The Lord has been again mindful of our need, and has sent us in the means to meet the demands of two days. Besides the 1l. 10s. which came in for rent, a brother gave me this morning two sovereigns, a sister from a distance sent it., and a brother, who spent this day with us, put 12s. 6d. into the box at my house, which our need soon brought out.

Nov. 23. This evening were given, after all the money had been again disbursed, 2 gold rings, 5 small silver coins, a silver ring, 5 silver studs, a silver buckle, a pair of ear-rings, a necklace, and a little box.

Nov. 25. As only 3s. 6d. had come in for knitting since the 22nd, we were now again very poor. The boxes in the Orphan-Houses were opened, but only 1s. was found in them. In this our poverty 6l. came in this afternoon for some of the articles which had been sent from Stafford on Oct. 3rd, and which had been sold some time since. This money had been expected for some time, but came in only now, in this our great need. In the evening came in still further 2l. from the East Indies.

Nov. 26. Today were sent from Newport, near Barnstaple, 2 rings, a brooch and 4s.

Nov. 27. This morning I received 4l. from a sister in Dublin, before we were really in need; but this donation came very seasonably to meet the large demands of tomorrow, Saturday, for which there is nothing in hand. There was also taken out of the boxes in the Orphan-Houses, this afternoon, 2l. 12s. 6d.

Nov. 28. Saturday. There has come in again 1l. today. Thus the Lord has bountifully supplied our need during this week, always sending the means without allowing us to be so deeply tried as during the two previous weeks.

Nov. 29. The Lord's loving hand has again today provided richly for the Orphans, for at least two days. There came in altogether 6l. 19s. 6d.

Dec. 1. Today we were so poor as to the Orphan-Fund, that we should not have been able to meet the demands of the day; but the Lord's loving heart remembered us. There came in this morning 5l. 7s. for some of the articles which were sent some time since from Stafford. I have purposely again and again mentioned how the help, which the love of some saints at Leeds and Stafford sent, delivered us, that it might be manifest that those donors were directed by the Lord in this matter.

Dec. 2. When today there was again but little money in hand, because of the disbursements of yesterday, D. C. brought me 2l., which his wife a sister had saved out of housekeeping, for the benefit of the Orphans. About an hour, after I had received this 2l., there was sent, in two post-office-orders, 6l. 4s. 6d. by a sister, being the produce of the sale of some trinkets; of which sum one half is to be used for the benefit of the Orphans, and the other half for my own personal necessities. Thus the Lord has by this donation also provided for myself and family, when we were in much need.

Dec. 5. Saturday morning. Yesterday afternoon a sister left two sovereigns at my house for the Orphans. The Lord in the love of His heart, remembered our Saturday's necessities, and sent in this supply; for there was only 18s. 6d. in hand when this money came, and 2l. 12s. is needed for this day. Evening. As there was now again only 6s. 6d. in hand, I gave myself to prayer, and immediately after I had risen from my knees, 1l. 5s. 6d. was given to me, for things which had been sold, being chiefly articles which had been sent from Stafford. There was also a flute left anonymously at my house, this evening.

Dec. 6. Today there came in still further 2l. 2s. 6d.

Dec. 7. Again 1l. 11s. has come in.

Dec. 9. Morning. This is the last day of the fifth year of the Orphan work. Hitherto the Lord has helped us! This morning there was only 1l. 1s. 9d. in hand, but 1l. 7s. was needed for the supply of today. I therefore opened the box in my house, in which 2s. 6d. was found. This 1l. 4s. 3d. I sent off to the Orphan-Houses. Evening. There came in during this day 1l. 6s. 6d.; out of this I had to pay away 1l. 2s., so that now, at the close of the year, though the balance amounts to 15l. 0s. 6 1/4d., there is only 4s. 6 1/4d. in hand, as the rest has been put by for the rent, which is due up to this time. With this 4s. 6 1/4d. we have now to commence the sixth year, leaning upon the living God, who most assuredly during this year also will help us in every way, as our circumstances may call for it.

At the close of these details (with reference to the year from Dec. 9, 1839, to Dec. 9, 1840) I make a few remarks in connexion with them.

1. Though our trials of faith during this year also have been many, and recurring more frequently than during any previous year, and though we have been often reduced to the greatest extremity, yet the Orphans have lacked nothing; for they have always had good nourishing food, and the necessary articles of clothing, etc.

2. Should it be supposed by any one in reading the plain details of our trials of faith during this year, that on account of them we have been disappointed in our expectations, or are discouraged in the work, my answer is, that the very reverse is the fact. Such days were expected from the commencement of the work; nay, more than this, the chief end for which the Institution was established is, that the Church of Christ at large might be benefited by seeing manifestly the hand of God stretched out on our behalf in the hour of need, in answer to prayer. Our desire, therefore, is not that we may be without trials of faith, but that the Lord graciously would be pleased to support us in the trial, that we may not dishonour Him by distrust.

3. This way of living brings the Lord remarkably near, He is, as it were, morning by morning inspecting our stores, that accordingly He may send help. Greater and more manifest nearness of the Lord's presence I have never had, than when after breakfast there were no means for dinner, and then the Lord provided the dinner for more than one hundred persons; or when, after dinner, there were no means for the tea, and yet the Lord provided the tea; and all this without one single human being having been informed about our need. This moreover I add, that although we, who have been eye witnesses of these gracious interpositions of our Father, have not been so benefited by them as we might and ought to have been, yet we have in some measure derived blessing from them. One thing is certain, that we are not tired of doing the Lord's work in this way.

4. It has been more that once observed, that such a way of living must lead the mind continually to think whence food, clothes, etc., are to come, and so unfit for spiritual exercises. Now, in the first place, I answer, that our minds are very little tried about the necessaries of life, just because the care respecting them is laid upon our Father, who, because we are His children, not only allows us to do so, but will have us to do so. Secondly, it must be remembered, that, even if our minds were much tried about the supplies for the children, and the means for the other work, yet, because we look to the Lord alone for these things, we should only be brought, by our sense of need, into the presence of our Father, for the supply of it; and that is a blessing, and no injury to the soul. Thirdly, our souls realize that for the glory of God and for the benefit of the church at large, it is that we have these trials of faith, and that leads again to God, to ask Him for fresh supplies of grace, to be enabled to be faithful in this service.

5. My heart's desire and prayer to God is, that all believers, who read this, may by these many answers to prayer be encouraged to pray, particularly as it regards the conversion of their friends and relations, their own state of heart, the state of the Church at large, and the success of the preaching of the gospel. Do not think, dear reader, that these things are peculiar to us, and cannot be enjoyed by all the saints. Although every child of God is not called by the Lord to establish Schools and Orphan-Houses, and to trust in the Lord for means for them; yet there is nothing on the part of the Lord to hinder, why you may not know by experience, far more abundantly than we do now, His willingness to answer the prayers of His children. Do but prove the faithfulness of God. Do but carry your every want to Him. Only maintain an upright heart. But if you live in sin; if you wilfully and habitually do things, respecting which you know that they are contrary to the will of God, then you cannot expect to be heard by Him. "If I regard iniquity in my heart, the Lord will not hear me: but verily God hath heard me; He hath attended to the voice of my prayer." Psalm lxvi. 18, 19.

6. As it regards the children of God, who by the labour of their hands, or in any business or profession, earn their bread, particularly the poorer classes of them, I give my affectionate yet solemn advice, to carry into practice the principles on which this Institution is conducted, as it regards not going in debt. Are you in debt? then make confession of sin respecting it. Sincerely confess to the Lord that you have sinned against Rom. xiii. 8. And if you are resolved no more to contract debt, whatever may be the result, and you are waiting on the Lord, and truly trust in Him, your present debts will soon be paid. Are you out of debt? then whatever your future want may be, be resolved, in the strength of Jesus, rather to suffer the greatest privation, whilst waiting upon God for help, than to use unscriptural means, such as borrowing, taking goods on credit, etc., to deliver yourselves. This way needs but to be tried, in order that its excellency may be enjoyed.

On Dec. 14, 15, 16, and 25, we had public meetings, at which the account of the Lord's dealings with us during the last year, in respect of the Orphan-Houses,

Schools, etc., was given, for the benefit of any who desired to come. The preceding part of the Narrative gives the substance of what was stated at those meetings, in reference to the many answers to prayer which the Lord has granted to us during the past year. There are a few points more, which may be of interest to the believing reader, and which were then mentioned, which I shall now add.

1. There have been, during this year also, six Day Schools for poor children, entirely supported by the funds of the Institution, all of which have been established by us.

Besides this, the rent for the school room of a seventh School, carried on by a sister, who is known to us, has been paid and two other such Schools, out of Bristol, have been assisted with Bibles and Testaments.

The number of all the children that have had schooling in the Day Schools through the medium of the Institution, since its formation, amounts to 2216; the number of those at present in the six Day Schools is 303.

These Day Schools have defrayed, by the payments of the children, about the sixth part of their own expenses.

2. There is one Sunday School entirely supported by the funds of the Institution.

3. There has been since the formation of the Institution one Adult School connected with it, in which, on the Lord's day afternoons, since that time, about 150 adults have been instructed.

This School has been discontinued at the close of this year, and instead of it it is purposed to have a regular Evening School for adults who cannot read. It is purposed to instruct them for about an hour and a half in reading and writing twice a week, and afterwards to read the Scriptures for a short time to them, and to bring the truth before them. The School will commence at seven o'clock in the evening, and the instruction will be altogether free.

4. The number of Bibles and Testaments which have been circulated through the medium of the Institution, during the last year, amounts to 452 copies.

There have been circulated, since March 5, 1834, six thousand and forty-four copies of the Scriptures.

5. There have been laid out during the last year, of the funds of the Institution, 120l. 10s. 2d. for Missionary purposes.

6. There are at present 91 Orphans in the three houses. The total number of the Orphans who have been under our care from April 11, 1836, to Dec. 9, 1840, amounts to 129.

I notice further the following points in connexion with the Orphan-Houses.

1. Without any one having been asked for any thing by us, the sum of 3,937l. 1s. 1d. has been given to us, as the result of prayer to God, since the commencement of the work. 2. Besides this also, a great variety of provisions, clothes, furniture, etc. 3. Though there has been during this year as much, or more sickness, in the Orphan-Houses, than during any previous year; yet I own to the praise of the Lord publicly, that it has been very little, considering the number of the children.

For the future we purpose, according to the time, means, etc., which the Lord may be pleased to give us, to attend to a fifth object, the circulation of such publications, as may be beneficial, with the blessing of God, to benefit both believers and unbelievers. We purpose either to buy or print tracts for unbelievers, and to sell them, or have them distributed, as opportunity maybe given; and to buy or print such publications, for circulation, as may be instrumental in directing the minds of believers to those truths which in these last days are more especially needed, or have been particularly lost sight of, and which may lead believers to return to the written word of God.

THE BLESSING OF THE LORD UPON THE WORK IN REFERENCE TO THE SOULS OF THE CHILDREN.

1. During the last fourteen months there have been meetings purposely for children, at which the Scriptures have been expounded to them. At these meetings an almost universal attention is manifested by them, which I thankfully ascribe to the Lord, and upon which I look as a forerunner of greater blessing.

2. During the last year three of the Sunday School children have been received into fellowship.

3. At the end of last year there had been eight Orphans received into communion: during the present year fourteen have been received: in all twenty-two.

4. Of those two who died during this year, one was an infant, and the other a girl about twelve years old. The latter, on the whole, a well behaved child, was for months ill in consumption before she died. The nearer she came to the end of her life, the greater was the solicitude of those under whose care she was, respecting the state of her heart, as she was evidently unprepared for eternity. But now we saw, what never had been witnessed in any other of the children to such a degree. This, on the whole, naturally amiable, meek, and quiet child, manifested not merely complete

indifference to the truth, the nearer she came to the close of her life; but also showed much aversion, and, as far as she could, great enmity to the truth. At last she was evidently dying, yet altogether unprepared for death. In this state all the Orphans in the Girls'-Orphan-House were assembled together, and the awful state of this dying child was pointed out to the unbelieving Orphans as a warning, and to the believing Orphans as a subject for gratitude to God on behalf of themselves, that they, by grace, were in a different state; and it was laid on their hearts to give themselves to prayer for their dying companion. The labourers in the work were sustained to hope still, and to pray still, though Charlotte Lee remained opposed to the truth while in this dying state. However, unexpectedly she lived ten days longer, and about two days before her death she was so altogether different, that we have hope in her end.

It was stated in the last year's Report, that we were looking for fruit upon our labours as it regards the conversion of the children, as the Lord had given to us a measure of earnestness in praying for them. The Lord has dealt with us according to our expectations. But I expect far more than what we have seen. While the chief object of our work has been, and is still, the manifestation of the heart of God towards His children, and the reality of power with God in prayer; yet, as we hoped, and as it has been our prayer, the Lord gives to us also the joy of seeing one child after another brought to stand openly on the Lord's side.--As far as my experience goes, it appears to me that believers generally have expected far too little of present fruit upon their labours among children. There has been a hoping that the Lord some day or other would own the instruction which they give to children, and would answer at some time or other, though after many years only, the prayers which they offer up on their behalf. Now, while such passages as Proverbs xxii. 6, Ecclesiastes xi. 1, Galatians vi. 9, 1 Cor. xv. 58, give unto us assurance not merely respecting every thing which we do for the Lord, in general, but also respecting bringing up children in the fear of the Lord, in particular, that our labour is not in vain in the Lord; yet we have to guard against abusing such passages, by thinking it a matter of little moment whether we see present fruit or not; but, on the contrary, we should give the Lord no rest till we see present fruit, and therefore in persevering, yet submissive, prayer, we should make known our requests unto God. I add, as an encouragement to believers who labour among children, that during the last two years, seventeen other young persons or children, from the age of eleven and a half to seventeen, have been received into fellowship among us, and that I am looking out now for many more to be converted, and that not merely of the Orphans, but of the Sunday and Day School children. As in so many respects we live in remarkable times, so in this respect also, that the Lord is working greatly among the children in many places.

I most earnestly solicit all who know the reality of our privilege as the children of God, even that we have power with God, to help us with their prayers, that many more of the children may soon be converted, and that those who have made a profession of faith in the Lord Jesus may be enabled so to walk, as that the name of Jesus may be magnified by them. The believing reader must know how great the aim of Satan will be to lead those children, who, from nine years old, and upward, have been received into fellowship, back again into the world, and thereby seek to lead believers to give up looking for real conversion among children.

The total of the expenses connected with the objects of the Institution, exclusive of the Orphan-Houses, from Nov. 19, 1839, to Nov. 19, 1840, is 622l. 2s. 6 1/2d. The balance in hand on Nov. 19, 1840, was 13l. 2s. 9 3/4d.

The total of the expenses connected with the three Orphan-Houses, from Dec. 9, 1839, to Dec. 9, 1840, is 900l. 11s. 2 1/2d. The balance in hand on Dec. 9, 1840, was 15l. 0s. 6 1/4d.

Dec. 23. There was sent to us for ourselves, anonymously, a piece of beef, which came very seasonably, as we are just now again very poor.

Dec. 26. This morning a poor brother, who, like ourselves, lives in dependence upon the Lord for his temporal supplies, whilst serving the Lord in the ministry of the Word, and who has been several days staying with us, gave to my wife 3s. 6d., for our own personal necessities, saying, that we might need it. This is indeed a most remarkable donation, both because of the individual from whom it came, and because of its having been given just now; for without it we should not have been able to provide for our temporal necessities this day.

REVIEW OF THE YEAR 1840.

I. As to the church.

68 brethren and sisters brother Craik and I found in communion, when we came to Bristol.

687 have been admitted into communion since we came to Bristol.

755 would be, therefore, the total number of those in fellowship with us, had there been no changes. But

79 have left Bristol.

55 have left us, but are still in Bristol.

44 are under church discipline.

52 have fallen asleep.

230 are therefore to be deducted from 755, so that there are only 525 at present in communion.

114 have been added during the past year, of whom 47 have been brought to the knowledge of the Lord among us, 24 besides, though they knew the Lord, had never been in fellowship any where; 43 had been at some time or other in fellowship, but most of them with saints not residing in Bristol.

II. As to the supply of my temporal necessities:

1. The Lord has been pleased to send me by the Freewill Offerings of the saints among whom I labour, through the instrumentality of the boxes L128 5s. 10 1/2d.

2. Through saints in and out of Bristol, by presents in money L100 5s. 1d.

3. Through family connection L8 18s. 0d.

4. In provisions, clothes, etc. worth to us at least L5 0s. 0d.

Altogether L242 8s. 11 1/2d.

Made in the USA
Lexington, KY
08 February 2017